GW00418150

A SERVING OF VERSE

I hope this very random read
Will fill your entertainment need

To Auriol.

Best wishes

Richard Garrard

A SERVING OF VERSE

Richard Garrard

Book Guild Publishing
Sussex, England

First published in Great Britain in 2012 by
The Book Guild Ltd
Pavilion View
19 New Road
Brighton, BN1 1UF

Typesetting in Bembo by
Ellipsis Digital Limited, Glasgow

Printed in Great Britain by
CPI Group (UK) Ltd, Croydon, CR0 4YY

A catalogue record for this book is available from
The British Library.

ISBN 978 1 84624 664 2

Contents

Part 1

Part 2

Part 4

Part One

Thoughts: (In a way)

Of all the creatures living in the world,
Man is most strange in many things he does.
He'll show compassion of the deepest kind
Or basely torture mind and body too;
Indeed, both qualities can oft be seen
To flourish greatly in the selfsame soul.
What animals, apart from but a few,
Who are considered base and low of life,
The reptiles, insects and strange water things,
Would set about to kill themselves *en masse*?
Most fights in nature, maybe to the death,
Are personally founded: not for all.
The family or tribe strives very hard.
Survival is its watchword all the time
And though a single member may fall foul
Of others that would pick a fight with them,
The social system must continue on
Against all odds, or everyone will fail.
If man would think this way and live as well,
Great benefits would flow. The truth to tell.

RICHARD GARRARD

To Jenny

'Tis time to thank you for the things you've done
To help me see my Kate, and now I've won
A wife restored to health and renewed strength,
Which will, I'm sure, last her for many years to come.
For when I meditate on 'might-have-been',
My own heart jumps a beat, as I had seen
Some dark and fearful times loom up on me
That seem would blot my future days, and cast
Great gloom upon my family.
To you I owe much comfort in these times
And hope this token that I now enclose
Will be a symbol of my gratitude.
And now I must rejoice with many friends
And look to future days that make amends
For much anxiety that's gone before.
Soon will our Kate be back in her real home.
I hope, with her, that you will to us come
And see yourself that she is really well.
It is a great relief: the truth to tell.

Promotion (Grandpa to Dad)

The birthday honours from the Queen
Did not include me in the scene,
But I was luckier than most:
A card came flying through the post
That brought an accolade most dear
And made me shed a joyful tear.
To think I've shed a generation
Gives me lots of motivation
To support what you have done
And all the prizes to be won.
So far you've shown your worthiness
To have a life full of success.
Make sure you know the things that matter
And build your own world from the clatter
That is around us all the time.
So then you'll have a life sublime.
Then let me say to you as well
You make us proud: the truth to tell.

A Cottager's Sunday
(A View of the Regency Run)

It were a lovely day,
I chatted with some friends of mine
As they were on their way
To be quite sure of their incline
To get their drinking place
Right close up to the bar,
Which gives them all the elbow space
To lift up jar on jar.
I joined them, later, for a beer
To show I was a friend,
But did not stay too long for fear
That rounds became a trend.
I thought I was all right to go
Back to my cottage door,
But stag'rin' filled me up with woe.
The distance seemed to be much more
Than I was used to see,
So, down the lane I took a rest
Beneath a big oak tree.
At my age it was for the best.
I must have dozed off for a while,
But suddenly came to.
I tried to climb up on the stile
It was a right to-do.
A galaxy of motor cars
Came roaring down the lane.
They rattled all the cow grid bars
And left an oily stain.
The front one wore a smile of chrome,
Which glittered in the sun.
I shall be glad to get back home

And have my teatime bun.
The normal things you see round here,
On Sunday afternoon,
Are riding folk and wild deer
Who don't appear so soon.
You've got a chance to say hallo
And get out of the way,
For life round 'ere is somewhat slow
In every kind of way.
As I was watching from my gate
The cars came to a halt.
I guessed the front ones had not ate
Or thought ajar of malt
Would help them on their merry way
When once they all got started.
It looked as if they all would stay
In case they should get parted.
It gave to me a lovely chance
To see the cars so near.
I had a good look, not a glance,
And shed a little tear.
The older cars took me right back
To when I were a kid
And all the gadgets they did lack
Were on the new ones, hid.
The drivers seemed to be quite pally
And proud of their old toys;
They told me they were on a rally
And spelled out all the joys
Of owning such a motor car
And having to prepare it
For these 'ere runs that go so far
To prove their work was worth it.
They said that they were Brighton bound,
Which seemed a little strange

7

With all the motorways around.
This lane will rearrange
The tyres, springs and chassis bits
And make the whole thing rattle;
The only transport that it fits
Is trailers full of cattle.
And then I found to my delight
That all the cars were named
The same, with badges polished bright,
And every bit was aimed
At giving pleasure at this sight.
Upon the finish line.

I realised that I could see
A great and wondrous thing
For all the cars were marked MG;
My heart began to sing.
And as they moved away from here
And musically purred,
I felt right proud that I'd been near
And had not been deterred.
It seemed as if I'd taken part
In mixing town and country,
Although it gave me quite a start,
I'll not forget the oak tree,
I'll even have a little stay
To help me with my mem'ry
Of all the things I saw today
On this momentous Sunday.

From Our Window

Our garden is a battleground
Where life is kept by chance.
You see the creatures all around
But closely look, don't glance,
And you will see 'control by size',
That sets the 'pecking order'!
The victims are the creepy things
That lose to the marauder.
The herring-gull scares all away
Though it is not aggressive.
The 'robin redbreast' tends to stay,
His cheek is most impressive.
The blackbird knows his way about
And thinks the bread is his,
But others bring his scheme in doubt
And put him in a tizz.
The starlings are like paratroops
That swarm down from the sky,
They guzzle every fruit that droops,
They then get up and fly
And sit up in the nearest tree
To get a better sighting
Of all the food that will be free
Within their close alighting.
My greatest friend of all the birds
Displays a speckled waistcoat.
His helpfulness is not in words
But deeds that make his mind gloat
Upon the hordes of snails that thrive
Among the plants and mush
Against which gardeners must strive:
He is, of course, the thrush.

The wren, the tit, the sparrow too,
The finch, the pigeon, crow and dove
All play their battle part and coo
In gardens that we love.

A Goddess in the Park

Are you misshapen as you seem to be,
Or is your beauty hidden from my eyes?
I do not know you, only what I see,
But were I nearer I may realise
Another view may make me change my mind.
In which case, I may have a sweet surprise
That puts my first impressions way behind.
Perhaps the anorak, a size too big,
The baggy jeans, the trainers and the hat
Are bits of clothing that I do not 'Dig'.
So must I turn away and say that's that.
But if I move a little to the left,
I may just catch a sighting of your face.
For when you hit an oyster on its cleft
A pearl appears quite snugly in its place.
Thus now a chiselled profile has appeared,
A sculpture of great skill and purity.
I now take back those thoughts that may have smeared
The truth that has so much dexterity.
At once you know that I am watching you,
And then you smile and both my legs go limp.
Beside the oyster I am but a shrimp.
Then can I see two emeralds in the pearl
Shining like stars up in a cloudless sky.
Your hat comes off to show off every curl
That makes an auburn cascade that does lie
Across your shoulders like a cape of gold.
You stand up and I need no more invent,
For what I see could not have been foretold.
I come towards you, full of good intent,
But someone else has come to take your arm;
And all my Venus leaves me is her charm.

Getting There

Time was when only birds could fly.
Now look and see what's in the sky.
A hundred years or so have past
When man first left the ground, at last,
To emulate the birds with wings
And build, with wires and sticks and things,
An aeroplane to go to places
Up, up and into empty spaces
Above the earth and oceans wide
And take, for man, a massive stride.
Travel in hours that once took days
By using his inventive ways.
A hundred years is but a wink
In world time only just a blink.
From one man taking quite a bet
To hundreds flying in a jet.
Look up again into the sky
And see the white trails passing by,
Ahead of each is just a speck
A tiny piece of world high-tech
At speeds not possible on earth,
Proving the great commercial worth
Of thought, design and sacrifice
That did result in this device.
Be it a jumbo or a Moth
A Concorde, Hercules or both,
The place to travel is the sky.
Faster and faster, by and by.
'Go west, young man!' and you will be
Ahead of time, you wait and see,
The Concorde hiccup cannot last,

Someone will want to go that fast
And cut the time down, way up there
By streaking through the stratosphere.
Propelled by rocket, maybe soon,
With tourist day-trips to the moon,
Cruising will not be on the sea
But round the planets: home for tea.
And what about the roads today?
The motor car has come to stay
And rapidly pursued its course
To totally replace the horse.
The key to transport's revolution
Is the engine's evolution.
One hundred years is all it took
To give world travel a new look.
Ten thousand years, or more, it seems
The horse and man have made up teams
To tackle any job there was.
They were the only power because
Materials, now 'everyday',
Lay hidden in a kind of way
That made them difficult to find,
But then we have to bear in mind
That 'NEED', the mother of invention,
Put many countries in contention
To satisfy consumer greed
And try to take a worldwide lead
By bringing to the population
Good things, that with manipulation
Of the way that they were carried,
Made Health and Wealth seem to be married.
And so we come to nowadays
When all this seems our normal ways
Of living out a busy life,

But bear in mind the depth of strife
That made the whole thing happen.

Give credit, also, to the train
That, in between times, took the strain.

The Twyford Ball Game

Come listen to the barks you hear in Berks:
It is the master catcher out at play.
The object of his frolics bears some marks
Which are inevitably there to stay.
The centre of the frenzy is a ball
Propelled by hand or foot across the ground.
You do not have to be so very tall,
But strong enough, of nerve, to stand the sound
Of orders coming from 'A man's best friend'.
This friend returns the ball right to your feet
And thus begins a process without end
Until you long to find a comfy seat.
Dream on! For you will not have time to stop
To wash the gunge off from your weary hand.
And woe betide you should your interest flop.
Such is the game played out in Oscarland.
The spur that keeps you going is those eyes
That sparkle with alertness and intent
Anticipation of a big surmise
Of where the ball is subsequently sent.
But if you have the slightest piece of luck,
Sweet Oscar may decide he's had enough;
Then hope the chance will come to pass the buck;
At least you'll feel, inside, you've done your stuff.

December the Twenty-Fifth

'Christmas comes but once a year,'
As we are often told.
It's meant to bring good tidings near
And keep us from the cold.
Great friendliness to all it brings
To many it's a bonus
But when it is attached with strings
It starts to be an onus.
When duty makes the family meet
To sing the lovely carols,
They try to keep their manners neat
Till someone taps the barrels.
The lubricant that flows from them
Makes dodgy situations;
It may create a lot of phlegm
Or vicious confrontations.
Toasts are meant to bring good luck
If full of Christmas spirit,
But sometimes they will score a duck
If someone is not 'with-it'.
Then Santa comes upon the scene
And children get attention
With presents, as it's always been
Back past a generation.
But Christmas really is about
A lovely birthday party
At which we all can sing and shout
And be both hale and hearty
To know about the one event
That changed the world for ever:
How one man, only three years, spent
Creating that which never

Has left us even though we went
Our own sweet ways sometimes;
His teaching drew us back to Him
To clear us of our crimes.
Restored in body, heart and limb
With hope that we will stay
Along the straight and narrow road
And never more will stray,
From following the Christmas code.

RICHARD GARRARD

Nightmares and Dreams

Here are some samples of my sleeping life.
There are some nightmares that come over me
That make me seem much poorer than I am.
I think my childhood gave me some deep fear
Of ending up in abject poverty.
The Great Depression from the General Strike,
A cocktail topped up with the Hitler War,
Had such a strong impression on my mind
That they have haunted me for evermore.
I dream of being without clothes to wear,
Of living in a sleazy B & B,
Or working in a rundown factory.
I'm climbing hills but never reach the top,
Alone and lost among the city streets.
The only contact with the human race
Is constables and railway station staff.
I've been on trains that never seem to stop,
On top of stairways that don't reach the ground,
I'm always feeling very much alone
And lacking money to support myself.
But in reality this is not so
For nothing I have written of this strife
Has happened to me in real life.

Apart from nightmares I have had some dreams.
For dreams can be quite pleasant at the time,
And fascinating too in many ways.
They can foretell what may about to be . . .
Once I dreamt whilst on a railway train
That there was going to be an accident
Halfway between the station and my home.
My car would hit a tanker full of fuel,

But when I got to where my dream had said,
It was not me but a white van instead.

At other times I levitate along,
Set in a sitting mode with legs outstretched.
I'm floating two feet up above the ground.
I travel quite a distance in this way,
It is a pleasurable way to move,
And quite a disappointment when one wakes
To lose that gliding feeling that it makes.

I never dream of anyone who's bad,
Or any real live action that I've had.
There seems to be a paranoiac aide
That fights my wish to always make the grade
To help my conscience guide me into ways
That find the best path through the worldly maze.
I wake up, and am very glad to find
That life for real has not been so unkind.

An Englishman's Castle

'A home' means comfort and tranquillity.
But look around the house and judge security:
You lock and bar the doors and windows too;
Alarms are set for anybody who
Would break in and create some big uproars.
But what is hidden in that fort of yours?
A host of hazards lurk within its walls:
There are things big and small that may cause falls;
If you have stairs, that is a dangerous place
For young and old, where terrors they may face;
A gate for toddlers, but the rest a rail
To help with balance should it seem to fail.
Downstairs you may delight in polished floors
And have a rug in front of all the doors;
The rug may trip you up or make you slip
And if you're lucky, only split your lip.
But greater damage can be done this way
Which may commit you to a ward-bed stay.
Now think of electricity supply,
And wall-plugs twenty centimetres high,
In reach enough to easily provoke
Those little fingers that would love to poke
Themselves, or any other thin device,
Into those slots. Result: Not very nice.
The kitchen is a horror place indeed
Where safety notices should make you heed
And understand what's right to do in there,
So that you take the necessary care.
Drawers full of knives and forks and poking things
That may cause many a wound that really stings.
The fingering of frozen food is such
That tender little hands could suffer much.

Beneath the sink, in cupboards you may find
Domestic chemicals that are unkind
To little people rummaging in there.
So, cupboard doors should be locked everywhere.
Now look around at hot things in this room,
And think about the horrors that may loom:
An oven that is halfway up the wall
Is better than one that is reached by all;
The greatest danger is upon the hob
Where saucepans busily perform the job
Of cooking food to feed the family,
And sit there boiling very happily.
But if the handles, on them, can be seen
From down below, it may make someone keen
To see what's in the saucepans; overhead;
They make one pull and nearly end up dead.
There is the kettle and the toaster too
That are part of the list that is taboo.
Let's go upstairs into the washing space –
There is a bath, and sink to wash your face.
But when the bath is full it's not a pool.
The water should not be so very cool
As to cause shivering from head to feet,
Nor should it be so very full of heat
That it can scald a very tender skin
And cause the sufferer to make a din.
But one important thing, you must agree,
Is depth of water of a low degree
As safeguard if the bather slips right down,
For humans have a tendency to drown.
This is enough to say inside the house . . .
The outside won't be quiet as a mouse:
An open front gate can be quite a scare,
But at the back you have to be aware

Of steps, a pond and spiky plants around,
If peace of mind is going to be found.
List all the dangers that you think might be —
Your castle, then, will be a sanctuary.

Dependence

Are you there?
Of course you're there,
You always are,
And to be fair
If you were far
My mood would be despair.
Dependence on you is much more
Than I had realised before.

What if you left?
I'd be bereft.
I'd be alone.
Oh there's a thought.
Get shopping in?
Be careful what I bought?
I bet I will be a disgrace
When bargain-hunting is a race.

The laundry bag.
The cleaning things.
The polishing.
The cooking times.
But, what to eat?
The bell of panic chimes.
Be calm, for all will be all right,
Though may not be a pretty sight.

Ah, there you are:
So, you're not far.
I had a fright:
You'd gone from sight.

I went quite white
To think that you had gone.
It hit me hard that I would miss
The part you play to make life bliss.

Time

What is the time?
How often have you heard that said?
There is a need to know the time
Or you are out of step instead,
For every thing is based on time.
When you are born you get a pack
Made up of time that starts to tick,
And no way can you turn it back;
You cannot make it slow or quick;
The speed of time is fixed for all.
It is the usage of your time
That makes it seem to fly or stall.
Misuse of time should be a crime,
For if you waste it as of right
That wastage never is retrieved.
Done to excess it is a blight
On blessings that could be received.
When you use every second of your pack
You will not have regrets when looking back.

Chair

My job is to provide you with some rest,
To sit upright or lie back well reposed.
My arms, my seat, my back are of the best
To comfort you or make you comatosed.
A mass of levers that you cannot see
Are working in me, and, at your command,
Will tilt you any way you want to be,
But press the button first, for your demand.
So! Are you sitting comfortably now?
Then I'll begin to tell a tale or two
Of why my history should take a bow.
I am a clone, not valued like a few,
No Hepplewhite nor Sheraton in me,
But, to be fair, they would not understand
My inner workings and machinery.
My frame is birch and little bits of steel;
Imagine, first, that I was once a tree,
And then, one day, I had that dreadful feel
That I was now a part of forestry.
So down I came and crashed upon the ground;
I was dismembered to make clones of chairs.
The feelings that I speak of can be found
Throughout the batch of seating that it shares.
So that is why what I say goes for all,
But wear and tear will vary on the way.
You may think stories that I tell are tall,
I hope they will amuse you if you stay.
At first, I must make comment of your weight:
It is exactly right for my design;
Some would be best described as freight
And stress me to where I would draw the line,
But voicelessness prevents me from a say.

Some sit down gently with polite finesse,
But others plonk themselves in such a way
That causes stretching and severe distress
To all my stitching and my webbing tacks.
I'd kick them off if I had half a chance,
And when they're bending give them well aimed whacks.
The things I fear the most are scratching cats —
They claw my sides and pull at the moquette,
But, then again, I hate unruly brats
Who wipe their trainers, even though they're wet,
Across my seat and arms without a thought
For others who would like to have a snooze,
And hope to find the chair that they have sought
Unmarked by mud and stains from lots of booze.
For me, a chair, I'd like to think, one day,
A hundred years from now I might be rare,
And be of antique value in a way
That calls for treating me with wondrous care.
The other option is to use me till
I end up with the others in landfill.

Compost

The autumn wind has done its work
And stripped the trees of golden leaves,
Thus letting sunlight to those spots
That suffer shade in summertime.
The tidy-minded have a task
To harvest all that's on the ground
For making compost for the spring.
The watchword of this modern age
Is to recycle all our waste.
'What's new?' you hear the diggers say,
Organic culture is a life
That gardens always have enjoyed.
Dead growth is so designed to fall
Around the root zone of all plants
To give the next year's 'hope of life'
To roots and seeds and all around.
Recover all that you can find –
Your garden will respond in kind.

Book

When picked up and my cover turned
The hope is that the turner learned
Much more than they did know before
Thus topping up their knowledge score.
My family is worldwide spread
And meeting some I rather dread,
The subject matter has a span
Of every class yet known to man –
From stark reality and fact
To fantasy devoid of tact.
There are relations who I know
With print that makes the reader glow
With shock to think an author can
Write down such things without a ban.
Romantic novels are quite nice,
But modern readers like to spice
Their lives with men and women who
Indulge in sex and rough stuff too.
A picture book will always be
A very pleasant thing to see.
Now when it comes to books at school
And each one is a learning tool,
The students have to take good care
They understand what's written there.
I've seen them looking at my page
With eyes full of frustrated rage:
They cannot join up what they've read
With anything the teacher said.
Philosophy, biography,
Arithmetic and history,
Geography and sciences
Are meant to build reliances

And personal ability
That forms a capability
To prosper in a chosen field
And gather up the greatest yield.
A string of languages and art
And drama studies as a start
To world renown and public fame
And beating others at their game.
Although a book is paper leaves
The type upon them simply heaves
With information crying out
To you to raise your voice and shout,
'EUREKA! All is clear to me,
My eyes are open, I can see.'
A book should always make some sense,
And authors are remembered hence
If they treat readers with respect.
For me, it is what we expect.

Migration

It makes you wonder what the future holds
When you can see confusion all around.
The balance of the whole world will unfold
As populations surge across the ground
Like ocean currents or a river bore,
A plague of locusts, growing more and more.
Large crowds of people showing great unrest
And packing up to find what they think best.
For many, disappointment will be where
They thought the grass was greener 'over there'.
Some others who appear to have won through
Have dislocated cultures they've gone to
Because they have not recognised the fact
That long traditions, if not left intact,
Will smoulder, with resentment, over time
And cause a stand to stop a rapid climb
In changes that bring fear and great distress
With prospects of an incoherent mess.
We hope that 'empire building' days are past
And countries now established will remain
At home to make communities that last,
Creating steadfastness that will not wane,
Administrations need the will to serve
And not abuse the privilege that's meant
To give their people all that they deserve
In welfare, which is never heaven sent,
But often is provided from outside
By bodies hoping to relieve the pain,
And help those people have a little pride
In self-sufficiency and lasting gain.
Some ruling bodies sometimes have the urge
To so arrange resources in their ken

To benefit their short-term need, and purge
Their consciences of fairness, as and when.
There seems to be a never-ending flow
Of goodies from soft-hearted folks abroad
Who find it difficult to really know
The real need for the things that they award.
They see the poverty and misery
And know that many things are not just right,
But shut their eyes to every vagary
That could build fortunes that are out of sight.
If justice in its fundamental sense
Could reign within the power-seeking mind,
The need for mass migration, here to hence,
Would cease to be a burden to mankind.

The Verse Maker

A poet, as you may suppose
Cannot express himself in prose.
He needs to find a phrase that flows
Around a subject that he knows,
And free the reader from his woes,
But never make him comatose.
In writing verse it always shows
Where word deficiencies arose.
The rhythm, haywire, sometimes goes.
A dodgy rhyme is one of those
Near fatal or destructive blows
That puts the poet into throes
Of deep despair down to his toes.
But he will very soon depose
The downbeat attitudes and close
His working day with writer's pose
To shout success, so that it shows.
Of critics he will soon dispose.
A poet sees beyond his nose.

RICHARD GARRARD

The Soul Seeker

I met a man the other day.
His soul was torn to shreds.
He wanted me to show the way
To pick important threads
Of thought relating to his life
And what may come beyond it.
He asked how he could ease the strife
And get, for him, a permit
To guarantee salvation now
From all that he has done.
I really could not tell him how
The goal he wants is won.
He could not choose what god he should
To give him all he needs,
For all of them profess and could
Reward him for good deeds.
But does he need religiousness
To help him sort his woes?
Or would just common steadfastness
Disarm his many foes?
The supernatural may seem
Traditional and right
To spell out an eternal dream
To someone out of sight.
But I was not the one to ask,
As I did try to tell him;
It was too big and hard a task.
In case I did deceive him.
I had to tell him truthfully
I did not have a god.
To me I live quite fruitfully,
Which seems to some quite odd.

34

The human mind has one big fault,
Which casts a spell of magic:
It's superstition and will halt:
Good commonsense. Quite tragic.

Why

The use of words has been researched for years,
But which ones are among those mostly used?
They must be AND or THE or A or BUT.
In grammar all such words are well defined,
But that is not the point of this survey.
There is a word that could take pride of place
Because it motivates the mind to think;
It wakes up men, creating greater things,
And every challenge that has ever been
Was started by a serious thought or dream
That follows this one word to make a seed,
An embryo or spark or starting point,
To make fictitious sciences come true . . .
Without it many questions don't exist.
In mind-flash or in writing or when said,
It sparks anticipation, joy or fear
Of what might follow it, just like a dog
All keyed up for the throwing of a ball.
Your ears are pricked and every nerve will try
To catch and understand what follows 'WHY' . . .

Limericks

There was a young man who played soccer,
But wanted to shine as a rocker.
He bought a guitar
But the noise was bizarre,
So his friends saved each ear with a blocker.

★ ★ ★

There was an old man in a bar
Who thought he had got there by car.
He looked for his keys
And he started to sneeze,
'It's the doctors I want, is it far?'

★ ★ ★

The fox that comes up to our door
Finds the food that we put out a bore.
It's always the same,
There's no fish and no game,
So he says he 'ain't coming no more'.

Muse Trouble

What is there left to write about
With all my muses dead?
My mind is like a lazy lout,
This fills me full of dread.
I wonder if the bards of old
Were ever in this fix —
When all the wordy trails go cold!?
They must have had some tricks
That started up their pens again . . .
But there are those who say
Verbosity creates a strain
So put those pens away.
Whatever subject that I chose
To make it stern or funny,
I had to quickly strike a pose
To give some worth in money.
The reader must obtain from it
A lasting satisfaction,
I hoped that it would be a hit
Not end in putrefaction.
Revamp my curiosity,
That keeps, my muse alive
And with renewed tenacity
My thoughts will start to thrive.
I only have to look around
Or hear what others say
To get my mind up off the ground
And, once more, let words play.

Limericks II

A man was bemoaning his lot –
Of money he had not a jot.
To make filthy lucre
He tried to play snooker,
But he found that his game went to pot.

★   ★   ★

Now every bee shows he has wings,
You see them on flowers and things.
He works in the hives
So the colony thrives,
But if you get too nosy, he stings.

A Tale of Two Garages

Two classic cars make lovely toys,
Though not when you must mend them,
Particularly if the boys
Have tendencies to bend them.
The servicing is easy stuff
When garages are double,
This means the cars are close enough
To cut out all the trouble
With marshalling the tools for both
Upon the same work bench,
For, when it's raining, you'd be loath
To find that missing wrench
That's always in the other car
That's garaged some place other.
It may be spanner or crowbar
That causes all the pother.
I know this problem well enough,
It's full of mad frustration.
My nerve ends get extremely rough
It's an abomination.
When we first moved into this house
There was a built-in garage,
I argued with my lovely spouse
But came across a barrage
Against a double one instead,
'For space would not allow'.
It, therefore, was put in my head
That if I would kowtow
To other things that must be done,
A larger lounge, in fact,
Another garage could be won

Which would not, then, detract
From frontal aspects of the site,
In fact it might improve
The balance of the roadside sight
And be the wisest move.
Impracticality unseen,
I have the true nightmare
Of two cars with a house between,
To others, please beware . . .
But it is not all doom and gloom –
If fitness is your thing,
Because of the restricted room,
Not for a cat to swing,
Your muscles will develop well
From getting round and under
With added exercise as well,
Created by the blunder
Of having to run over there
To get what you've forgotten
And find that it is over here
Because foresight is rotten.
Two sets of tools may fit the bill,
But that is not an option,
So press on with determined will
And show that your adoption
Of better ways will give the thrill
Of RE-ORGAN-ISATION.
The trouble is, each garage holds
More than a car and bits;
You stand there with your arms in folds
To gather up your wits.
One day my son gave me a tip –
'Don't sort your garage, get a skip!'

Ode to Sailing

Oh what a lovely feeling it can be
To cast off and be absolutely free,
And watch a cloud of billowing sails above
Persuade your ship across the sea you love.
The gentle undulation of the waves
Creates that relaxation each man craves.
It is a wondrous feeling, no mistake,
To watch the bow wave lead the trailing wake.
A wind increase will roughen up the ride
And all the time you must respect the tide,
But if your ship is sound she'll meet the swell
And rise up to this challenge just as well.
In modern times, each sailing ship has props
To carry out manoeuvres where it stops;
They're also very handy when at sea
If wind is always blowing you to lee.
There is one magic moment in all this
That brings about exhilarating bliss:
It is, when you have left port under power,
And seen astern the harbour lighthouse tower . . .
With all the necessary sails well set
The wind is filling them and then you get
The order to 'Cut engines'. That is bliss,
That is the moment nobody should miss;
The silence is remarkable just then,
For this is that sweet time, and only when
You first will hear the orchestra of sound
That makes a sailing ship beloved wherever bound.

Finale

Don't mourn for me,
Or I shall haunt you.
Don't cry for me,
Or I shall haunt you.
No incantations at my death,
Or I shall haunt you.
Dispose of me the simplest way,
Or I shall haunt you.
Tell not the world that I have gone,
Or I shall haunt you.
If you think well of me,
And can remember me,
I will not haunt you.

Words

What funny things some people say —
Their origins are far away
And many are just wordy play,
An inner meaning goes astray,
Some mentioning the time of day.

The mottos, clichés, proverbs, puns
Depend on how the wording runs.
It is important that it stuns
The reader with the wordy guns
To understand the clever ones.

'Ne'er cast a clout till May be out.'
But who is going to have that clout?
Perhaps it really is about
Some clothing on someone who's stout,
Not nice for May to see without.

'A dripping June sets all in tune.'
From what wise tree has this been hewn?
I guess that June will be immune
From fever if her clothes are strewn
And dried to songs to her fortune.

A motto is a smart device
To give to all succinct advice
In fewest words that will suffice
To tell the reader to be nice
To those involved, at any price.

The metre of this verse is different and coy,
For a cliché will always be sure to annoy,
Because it's designed to repeat the same ploy,
It's often discarded as you would an old toy.
But it may be the truth that you should not destroy.

A play on words will make a pun.
I wish I knew a clever one.
My thought clouds have obscured my sun,
My word manipulation done.
Perhaps my score was always none.

So here I've tried to you explain
The weakest link in every chain
Is that which cannot take the strain,
But don't forget 'No pain, no gain'.
I hope I've made that very plain.

Review

When I look back at all the things I've seen,
And couple that with all the things I've heard,
A massive canvas is required to show
The fullest details of the life I've had.
Is luck, good fortune or coincidence
As real an influence along the way?
Some choices are deliberately made;
More often, though, I was not free to do
What I thought was the right and proper thing.
A forceful circumstance surrounded all
And I was wary of a tragic fall.

The balance of the things I did achieve
Was topped up in the cocktail of my life.
The main ingredients were those of moods
That showed the world the state of mind I had.
Serenely calm or loudly shouting out
Told to all others if approach was wise.
When I saw chances of a better deal,
And had to put my trust in someone else,
I tried to clear my mind of any doubt,
For when my handshake showed the way ahead,
I could not, then, want something else instead.

The bow of living sees the rocks ahead
And helmsmanship will keep the sea at bay.
The wake can only tell me where I've been
But also carries flotsam best forgot.
And as the troubled sea calms down again
The hope is that the flotsam won't become
The jetsam on some beach a long way off
And lurk about to be a real lee shore,
Or minefield that will catch me unawares.
I'll try to steer a cautious-minded course
With but one object: to avoid remorse.

Watch It!

A lovesick youth will get much sympathy,
But when he puts on sixty years or so
Tradition says he's lost his empathy –
This is not so: he can get up and go.
Ability is there that needs some time
To get the heart strings harping out the tune
That fits the words and generates the rhyme
To let the old man cease to be a prune.
Old dogs are not supposed to learn new tricks
But they have got great knowledge on their side.
And two and two makes five when they can fix
A formula that's come from far and wide.
Don't underestimate what you can see,
There's still a need for deepest sympathy.

Beauteousness

Can anyone describe to you what beauty means to all?
Beholders are supposed to know what gets them hooked and fall.
It is not only with your eyes that you can beauty find;
Your ears may play a bigger part in making up your mind.
A piece of stone, a block of wood, so fashioned by a hand,
That it remains a lovely piece that all can understand;
And so it stays for evermore admired without change.
But living things are different and prone to rearrange
Their better features, big or small, maturing with the years.
A person's face, for instance, can be masked against the fears
Of changing looks that may disclose the real facts of their age.
And then you read, in Shakespeare, that the whole world is a stage.
So everything you look at could be false or make-believe,
And those who show you beauty may be laughing up their sleeve.
For me, I think delightfulness is bound up in a mood
Of happiness and friendliness and willingness to brood
Upon the well-known pleasant things that I can see around
That spell out pure simplicity with sympathetic sound.
And when I look at natural things like flowers and fruit and trees,
I am in awe of colour and of perfect symmetries.
To me it always is a fact that what looks right is right,
But this is just the 'skin-deep' thing that's based upon my sight.
For lasting deep attraction for one person to another
Lies not in looks that may well fade and cause a lot of pother.
It is the eyes that show the soul and deepest attitudes
And, with the voice, the whole transcends the basic platitudes.

The Mirrored Lady

Reflections of the way you look
Are very seldom 'copy-book'.
A mirror is a truthless thing:
It shows you only fantasy;
It will not nor it cannot bring
To you your real live legacy.
Your image to those round about
Can never be the same as yours,
Because they see you, without doubt,
Complete with all your many flaws,
The wrong way round to what you think.
The only way, you may suppose,
To make your image have some link
With fashion is to change your pose
With paints and cuts and clips and curls.
A face-lift sometimes does the trick,
But don't forget the string of pearls
That will help you to look quite slick.
Be cautious, though, for when it's done
Your friends may not know who you are.
In which case, you will not have won
Improvement that you should, so far.
It would be best to start again.
Back to the drawing-board, they say,
Assuming that you can regain
Your first appearance in a way
That all your friends will recognise.
So settle for the face you've got
And with some subtle compromise
You'll probably achieve a lot.
Before you curse the mirrored form,
Set up two mirrors, more maybe.

Reflect reflections to inform
You of the view that others see.
You're bound to get a great surprise.
You're better than you realise.

Putting Your Hands Together

There is a sound that's made in many lands.
It can be loud or soft: it's clapping hands.
In praise, in warning or in mild shock,
It is a language all will know *en bloc*.
It needs no words to pass intent along,
Reaction is immediate and strong.
You can enforce the message with your face:
In praise you smile; to scold you will grimace.
To slowly hand-clap is a warning sign
Of great frustration getting out of line.
A single clap will make a local sound
To scare a bird or reprimand your hound.
A child may come to order with this noise
And, hopefully, adopt a better poise
More suited to the company they're in
So that they lose the title of urchin.
Applause is the most common use of claps –
If done with vigour it, quite soon, entraps
All those around to add their praise as well,
Rewarding good performances, and tell
Their fellows that they have a wish to show
That body language has the words all know.
But if the clapping message is so clear
And has been understood by human ear
For million upon million years, we'll say
This piece I've written could be called *passé*.

Forgiveness

What if you were a victim of a crime?
Would you be merciful towards the one
Who hurt you or destroyed your property?
It is a major testing time to bear.
For there are two extremes that show themselves:
A deep resentment fills your troubled mind,
Instinctively your thoughts turn to revenge
To compensate for all the damage done;
The other of the two views of your plight
Is not to bring a charge but to forgive:
But law allows severest penalties
To fit the evidence displayed in court
And, as a citizen within the law,
Your duty is to turn wrongdoers in.
The fuzzy area between these points
Allows vast argument for clemency.
What of the person standing in the dock?
Their hope is surely one of liberty;
We must assume that felons always think
That they will not be captured for their sins;
But when they are, do any show remorse?
Not when the fuzzy area displays
So many ways of weighing up the crime.
It is a pack of cards to shuffle with
Until the answer that you need comes up
To give 'Not Guilty' or the lowest penalty.
Consider, for a while, who can forgive.
The victim may declare an amnesty
For fear that vengeful attitudes are there.
Long memories are tricky to erase
On either side, when souls are not at rest.
The hurt will never really go away.

It is the perpetrator who must sweep
Away the stains upon their character.
To get this done they must forgive themselves.
It's no good asking for a god to help –
Self-help is all that satisfies the case.
Reprogrammed minds must come from deep inside
If sinfulness will no more there abide.

Within a close relationship there is
A very different atmosphere than crime.
The comment with sarcasm as its aim,
The cynical remark, the bitten lip,
All these can be more harmful than some crimes.
The circumstance of living in a group
With family connections, man and wife,
Leaves very little room to heal the wounds
When character assassins are at work;
For frequent contact jogs the memory
And reconciliation has no chance,
Unless the harasser can come to terms
With all the mental anguish they impart.
Their souls and consciences should quickly be
Detached from all the trappings of the world
By their own hands and rigorously cleaned
In, what might well be called, a Glory-bath.
Then would the vicious tongues be ripped away
And chances of forgiveness made more real.
Offenders, first, must show the flag in this
Before they can expect the victim's smile.
Then will the sinners clear their minds of sin
And peacefulness will be the goal to win.

Ode to the Fox

Oh pretty fox, oh wary fox.
Your cunningness is better known,
The way you run rings round the flocks
Of hunters, who, with dogs, bemoan
Their inability to catch
A sight of you; for just a glance
Would justify a 'down the hatch',
When after-stories get a chance
Of credibility and form a batch
That adds to folklore, country-wise.
In towns your life may have less stress,
But daily menus, I surmise,
Need more discretion, I would guess,
But there are some of humankind
Who put out food so that you could,
With sight and smell, quite freely find
More easily than rabbits would.
Unique abilities you own
Make you a cross between two pets.
By looking like a dog, alone,
Endears you to the doggy sets,
But catlike you can scale a wall
Or sunbathe on a handy roof.
In wildlife you have got it all,
Intelligence is yours as proof.
I'd love to have a fox to pet.
It's not impossible, they say,
But if you listen to a vet
It must be trained from its first day.
Perhaps it would be rather wrong
For it would, for its freedom, long.

Once Upon a Doorstep

Why is this fellow lying there like that?
This man with baking foil for a hat.
How did he choose this doorway for a home?
The symbol of his kingdom is his dome
Surmounted by a shining silver crown.
But why does anybody get so down?
The reasoned history of such a state
Might show a thousand things upon his plate
Of life that he may wish to be unknown.
For him, the winds of fortune have not blown
His argosy to harbours full of gold.
It may be that he was not very old
When bare survival was the way to go.
Tycoon or drop-out, we may never know –
If we pass by and think of him no more
We will not add to our 'compassion' score.

But whilst the blood is coursing through his brain,
There must be some way to undo the chain
Of time-events that could have put him here
To live a life that seems to have no fear.
The coloured duvet indicates some taste,
Or was it stolen from the nearest waste?
The foetal attitude he now displays
Could be reflected thoughts of mother-days.
More likely, as all animals of old,
He's curled up, merely, to keep out the cold.
To make his mind up for him, we might guess
His type of freedom is not such a mess,

Though we, in houses, do not think it bliss.
We think of hostels, but we may just miss
That 'private lives' are personally owned
And privacy is neither bought nor loaned.

Although the laws of sleeping rough are clear,
A peaceful doss will not draw conflict near.
No doubt the doorstep sleepers have a code
That each respects in diplomatic mode.
The hidey-hole that has been shown as theirs
Remains in ownership devoid of cares.
Who knows? Our sympathy may be misplaced.
He may have made another feel disgraced.
To wake him would invoke a bad mistake,
It would be funny if he's just a fake,
But by the look of him he's real enough.
I'm not the one to try to call his bluff.
And having passed and left him lying there,
I'll always wonder: should we show more care?
A lifestyle chosen is the aim of all,
But tread you carefully: one trip: you fall.

Doggerel

I saw a man go down our street,
He held a leash looped round a dog,
And as we closed enough to meet
The dog looked like a furry log.
I chatted with the man a while,
But it was very clear to see
The dog had no good cause to smile
And only wanted to be free.
He stretched out on the paving stones
As though caught in an endless trance,
His dreaming must have been of bones
And praying also for a chance
To run and run and run and run,
To catch a ball and bring it back.
He'd relish the enormous fun
That walking endless pavements lacks.
The man, the dog and I went on
And reached the supermarket door.
The man said, 'I'll see you anon.'
He made the dog sit on the floor
Outside and tied him to a post.
The man went in. I thought, that's rough.
For some strange reason, unlike most,
I lingered and did hear a gruff
And saddened voice come from the dog:
'See what it's like, it's no surprise
For you to realise the slog
It takes for him to recognise
The most unnatural loyalty.
Don't listen to the bosh you hear
Of owners' mystic royalty.
I do his bidding more from fear

That feeding time will be no more.
He's not the leader of the pack
As you are told, he's just a bore;
I'm ne'er supposed to answer back.
It's all right if I am resigned
To push my instincts out of sight,
But doggy lives were not designed
To never growl or never bite.
My claws and teeth are never used
For catching and devouring prey.
The fire within me is defused.
Look at me, this is my whole day.
From puppyhood I've been brainwashed
To be a "Thing" for company.
To toe the line and not get coshed
For but the slightest felony.
My breed debars me from real work
That stretches mind and muscle too.
I'd never feel the need to shirk
From duties that I'd love to do.'
Just then the man came back again
And took the leash and walked away.
The dog walked on and did not strain.
Our talk will, with me, always stay.
The dog looked back and winked an eye –
It took my willpower not to cry.

Pairing

I think of you the moment that I wake,
I think of you with every breath I take,
I think of you with every step I make.
My finding you has not been a mistake,
My love for you has never been a fake.
When I look back across decadal years
And how I disarmed all my passing fears,
I wonder at the way my life appears
To others who are harassed by their peers.
Good luck? The cloud in my sky always clears.
A cycle ride into the countryside
Was the fair wind that turned a friendly tide.
And then, beneath a tree so tall and wide,
You let me kiss you, and I burst with pride.
Such moments are the sweeter if they hide
From public view, locked in the memory:

Then started the evolvement of two lives
With little doubt that such a thing survives
When each one of a pair, with will, contrives
To make the pair be one, which then revives
The freshness upon which the pairing thrives.
I know that I've been luckier than most
And in my heart of hearts I tend to boast
About my clear emergence from the host
Of others racing for the winning post
To gain your company. Now here's a toast:

To all that has been and will so remain,
My gratitude is endless for the gain.

The Egg and Sperm Race

We're asking why our lives were thrown away
And why we never had the chance to stay.
To come together was a tricky thing –
It gave us both an even bigger zing
To find a corner in a cosy womb,
Not knowing that it would become our tomb.
We're speaking as one lost and lonely soul
Cut down before we reached our first great goal
To breathe fresh air and see a wondrous world
And have our body, like a flag, unfurled.
Who knows? We might have been someone of fame
If we had been allowed to join the game
Of living with the others of our kind,
And given to the world a mastermind.
There's tens of thousands of them, all like us
Who've suffered termination without fuss
And left to ponder through eternity . . .

Some say we have no soul before we're born
And that's an argument that is well worn.
Conception means an embryo is there
And, with a lot of thought and loving care,
Will get to life's great stage that all call birth.
The early teens will show the body's worth
To pass the final test to be adult
And pour out blessings to the human cult.
The medics may have reasons to abort,
But ancient ethics mean that we are taught
That killing is a dreadful thing to do;
Unless to save a life, it is taboo.

In every case, if healthiness prevails,
Sweet nature must be eased through the travails
To nurture living things at any cost,
Or prospects of the world will all be lost.

Life's Ups and Downs

It was one day in May
When you held me at bay,
Until I said that I would love you for ever.

You later let me stay,
We made a vow that day
That our parting was never but never but never.

There is a valid way
To fend off an affray,
To have wits about you and be a bit clever.

If there's a time to pray
Be careful what you say,
You make a mistake and you'll see good bonds sever.

You do not need display
To make your efforts pay,
As for my love for you there's no doubt whatsoever.

Life has a way to sway,
To stop it you belay
The tangled up ropes that will pull you wherever.

We've heard of feet of clay
That tend to go astray,
So push on the brakes of your conscience whenever.

If things come on a tray
Beware that they may flay
The very back off of your greatest endeavour.

Now put the gloom away
And have a day of play,
So cast off your troubles; be happy for ever.

Felidae

A picture of a kitten on our wall,
A photograph in black and white, that's all.
Some may think it is very dull to see:
The frame is black, the white mount seems to be
Four times the size of feline portraiture,
But this ignores the life-full aperture,
That ball of fur, demanding eyes and ears
Draws your attention, fills you full of fears
That, if you look away, the claws may flash
And catch you unawares: inflict a gash.
All cats of any size are autocrats,
But, hopefully, this one is not like cats
Who dance a jig before they make a spring,
And have no gratitude for cosseting
But glides, emerging with a tuneful purr.
Such majesty is never with a cur.

If it's a kitty, she will love a pet,
But if a tom-cat, he will need a vet.
The more I look into that kitten's eyes
The more my enigmatic thoughts arise.
I have to turn away to clear my mind
And fight mesmeric feelings that I find.
My main dilemma is the place I sit
To watch the television, which will fit
In no place else because of furniture,
And when I lift my eyes the miniature
Sweet furry puzzle keeps an eye on me.
But all is well if only joy I see.
The picture of the kitten on the wall
Will always be beloved by one and all.

The Clipper

The other day I walked through Greenwich Park.
A lovely day with lovely things to see.
The one great treasure, though, is *Cutty Sark*,
A statement of how travel used to be.
She lies there as if ready to set sails,
But she's restrained by struts and blocks and walls.
No longer are longshoremen heaving bales,
For now her living comes from her gift stalls.
I left the park and entered busy streets,
And as I browsed I found the market hall.
Two women haggled over linen sheets,
Two men were leaning up against a wall.

As I passed by one man said to the other,
'Have you been down to see that old-time boat?
Those bits of wood and rope would cause a pother
If tangled up when it had been afloat.
To think that thing could cross the seven seas
And travel at the speed they say it did.
It must have been a bit more than a breeze.
It's hard to take it in, to be candid.'
I intervened and tried to be polite
When telling them the right words to be used
For all the things that came within their sight.
I thought their concept seemed to be confused.

I started gently on the wordy trip.
'To start with,' I said, 'it is not a boat
But a prime sample of a full-rigged ship.
No bits of wood or tangled rope, you note,
But yards and booms and sprits and masts to bear
The force developed by the wind-filled sail.

Controlling sheets to guard against a tear
In vital canvas if allowed to flail.
The ropes are stays and sheets and halyards too,
The sails are courses, gallants, stuns and jibs,
Topsails and royals reaching to the Blue,
A crossjack and a spanker top "His Nibs".'
'Now, as you stand here when the wind is strong
You hear a whistled melody above,
The rigging brings back memories in song
That every sailorman has learned to love.
But standing here you cannot hope to feel
The movements of a sailing ship at sea.
These are addictive; have a strange appeal,
You soon know there is nowhere else to be,
But in this graceful creature, letting you
Be, as a guest, within her loving care,
Rocked in a cradle with a mother's coo.
Of course, the ocean was not always fair.

'Think "watery graves". A thousand miles from home
Without a single chance of help to come.
So, trading forces outweighed risks to roam,
And those who gained from it were glad that some
Were brave enough to tame the sea and wind
With such a lovely thing we call a ship;
Competing with the creatures that are finned
And travel well below the surface whip.
The downside that you cannot replicate
Is swaying rigging and the shouts below
At men way up aloft, as ordered by the Mate
To shorten sail to meet the coming blow.

'They clawed at canvas till their fingers bled
And if a man should fall: no turning back.
A lifebelt would be little use instead,
He'd bob there; knew the ship would never tack.
And standing here, whilst I relate this tale,
You never will hear tragic screams of men
Flung by the shipboard seas against the rail,
But only calls for ice-cream, now and then,
Or screams of laughter from the milling crowd.
So spare a thought for those who sailed in her,
This graceful monument without a cloud
Of canvas on her spars, as She'd prefer . . .

'Look up at all the cordage, neatly rigged,
And, hopefully, you've got a better view
Of what this dear old Lady means, and twigged
The purpose of her being here for you.'
They thanked me for the information gained,
I thanked them for the patience that they set
And felt their interest had, in no way, waned.
We said goodbye and parted where we met.
I walked back up the hill in Greenwich Park,
But had to look back down to *Cutty Sark*.

Clock

The face that haunts is one that tells the time.
The hands that show the time control our fate.
There is no way that we can turn them back.
The Cyclops eye that comes straight out at us
Gives focus to the centre of the dial;
The hands assume the strength of giant's arms
That force each millisecond of our lives
Into the history of all the world.
Before the clock, there was sweet dawn and dusk,
A moment chosen, by fatigue, to rest,
A random interval to search for food
When instincts told our bodies to refuel.
Our growth would reach a stage when we could tell
That 'needs must' prompted us to find a mate.
And so the species moved on to the days
When 'order' had to be the way of things
And 'dawn to dusk' became a chunk of time;
Though darkness had to be a part of it.
So, when could one day start and one day stop?
The concept of some kind of time was born.
A day would be made up of equal parts
Beginning in the middle of the night,
But why was twenty-four the sum of them?
And why was twenty-four split into two
To make two half-days each composed of twelve?

And so was stress invented for mankind.
To give some order out of chaos seemed
To be of universal benefit.
But keeping time brought hurt where there was none.
And competition raised its ugly head,
Egged on its way by every ticking clock,

Until the sound, like timpani, increased
To fever pitch to brainwash everyone
Into a lifestyle that would seem to be
Quite normal, though, in actual fact, it was
A lasting brainstorm whirling round and round
So that, with everything we say or do,
We must keep time with everybody else.
The very part of us that gives us life,
Our heart, is said to be in healthy nick
When beating measures right against a watch.
That brings to focus what we do all day.
That thing upon our wrist is aptly named:
We're always 'watching' time in case we're late.
But, late for what?

Too late to reach our goals before we die?
The goals may be a dream to anyone.
Ambition rarely fits our own true skill,
But time is wasted on these dreams of ours.
In order to survive in modern times
We must conform to have the slightest chance
To make a mark along with our own kind.
Just flick the coin and we are sure to find
The other side will make it very plain:
Make friends with CLOCK to make the greatest gain.

The Telephone Call

I never really thought of that.
It never even crossed my mind,
But now that you've reminded me
It would be churlish and unkind
Of me to claim I did not see
The point of what you said last night.
I must say it's a big surprise,
But I expect you are quite right
To question such an enterprise.
I find it difficult to think
That anyone would keep that dark;
It will, of course, cause quite a stink
When sleeping dogs wake up and bark.
How will they straighten all this out?
You sound concerned about the cash,
But what about the laws they flout?
The whole shebang will turn to trash.
Please say that you are not involved,
Your livelihood would be at stake.
Let's hope they soon get it resolved
And save you from a big mistake.
I wish that I could help in this
But all my skill would not suffice
To turn this problem into bliss
Or make it even seem quite nice.
You're right, the timing was not good,
A little later on, maybe,
When things may seem as if they could
Give all the clarity to see
The broader aspect – way ahead –
And count the chickens when they're hatched,
But hindsight is no help instead.

71

You're always stuck with chances snatched.
Will all the assets have to go?
You said he'll have to leave quite soon –
He'll have to leave his house? Why so?
To have him near has been a boon.
I guess I've lost the plot somewhere.

You mean the firm is not at risk?
And nothing will be changing there?
I see: you mean, if he should go,
Commercial confidence may dip?
A 'one-man band', as you will know,
Depends upon an ego-trip.
What's that you say? That sort of bloke?
I thought you meant the firm was broke.
Good heavens! What with all my chat
I never really thought of that.

Let's Go a Musing

When sweet Erato gives me company,
A sentimental mood wells up in me
And I can only think of your fair face
That glows with loveliness and charming grace.
My love for you transforms to poetry
Which tries to give the picture symmetry

To meet Urania gives food for thought.
The stars will then hold sway, we're always taught,
And tell us how the universe was formed
To give our sun the power, we are warned,
For good or evil on our planet earth,
But we must find the astronomic worth.

Melodic tones are hoped for when we hear
The muse Euterpe will be coming near.
The sounds called music do not always please,
They can both drive you mad or put at ease
Your twanging nerve strings needing longed-for rest
If you have been bombarded by the zest
Of pop or ragtime or some lively jazz
Created with the loving razzmatazz.
For me, some jazz is well constructed fun,
But lilting airs feed soul and mind as one.

What fun it is to have Thalia call.
So many talents helping one and all
To have a happy and a beauteous life,
And, with her sister Graces, care and strife
Are banished as the mist before the sun
To show us comedy, with rivals, none.

Call Clio up and you will see the past
And get perspective of the world at last,
More clearly than you've ever seen before,
Relating history without a flaw.
Let Polyhymnia now have a say,
And bring a solemn theme to our whole day
With sacred songs and poetry and mime
That bring tranquillity at any time.

Calliope will set a mammoth task
With words of grace and nobleness that ask
You to believe, quite deeply, as you read
Of every wondrous happening and deed
That can be dramatised in Epic form
To leave the world a masterpiece to warm
The hearts and minds of all romantic souls
Who never reached their most ambitious goals.

A most foreboding meeting, now, for you.
It's sad Melpomene, to tell you true,
Grim tales of human suffering and grief.
It seems no matter how we duck and weave,
We're touched by Tragedy that makes us grieve.
It may be near, it may be far away,
But some disaster happens every day.

The last of all nine muses to appear
Is Terpsichore to belay your fear
That ups and downs in life are all too real.
So, now put on your dancing shoes and reel,
Sing out full volume, let the chorus sound;
Forget your troubles, let full life abound.

Follow My Leader

It was a lovely sunny day in May.
I sat upon the terrace chair to see
The world go by and find my part in it.
I looked in meditation at the slabs
That neatly fit together so to form
A level walkway for an even tread.
A thousand thoughts whirled round within my mind.
Then, suddenly, my eyes fixed on a slot
Between the slabs that were not quite closed up.
A tiny creature busily emerged –
Its confidence encouraged more to come,
And soon there was a milling crowd of them,
Each with a special job to go and do.
Quite soon an ordered state of things appeared
And lines of workers holding grains of sand
To fill the slot between the paving-stones.
I looked and looked and gazed in wonderment;
I was transfixed upon the thing I saw.
Hallucinations overcame my mind
And I began to float up in the air
As though ballooning in the countryside.
The moving lines of regulated ants
Transformed into a teeming motorway
That snaked its way across the fertile land.
The convoys of the never-ending cars
Were mixed in with the never-ending trucks
All seeming to have but a single aim,
As do the ants in their determined way.
'But think again and ponder on the scene',
I had to tell myself, as on I watched.
The river of tin cans on wheels flows on

Because each can contains an independent soul
With independent thoughts of where to go,
Each hoping they will get there in the end.
A general purpose may be well assumed,
But this could not be further from the truth.
The only reason why they travel thus
Is fencing that restricts the general spread.
The ants keep line without such barrier.

The single-minded driver only hopes
That at the end of it there'll be a space
To park the tin can out of reach of law.
He, then, will go about his purpose there,
Competing, all the time, with his own kind.
Is ant-life freedom or autocracy?
Each one is certain what it's meant to do;
Perhaps a democratic way is there
Unseen by us who are so far away.
Research will tell how all the ants behave,
But what is in their minds, down under there?
It must be true that living things have thought,
They must have memories to stay alive
And know what's good to eat and how to breed;
They know how to survive and where to hide.
And as I stared and only traffic saw
I did not feel a part of it at all.
The ants, the cars, the constant to and fro
Has little bearing on the world at large.
The tides, the weather and the seasons all,
The vegetation and the heating sun
Shrug off the influences made by man,
And all the freedom living creatures have
Is tolerated for a little while,
And disappears amid the mists of time.

Hallucination gone, I found myself
Upon the selfsame chair I was before.
The motorways had disappeared from view.
My close companion ants still plied their trade.
I had to rack my brains for reasons new
To find out the result my thinking made.
Press on and hope that I have done my stuff
And pray that what I've done is good enough.

Every Hamlet's Choice

Two Bs or not Two Bs? That is the question.
Or is it better, in the end, to suffer
The swings and roundabouts of private gain
Or kill our qualms with true Democracy?
To lie, to creep would be an ostrich choice,
But if we creep we'll surely hear the Blare,
That trumpet call that will dispel all fears,
And make us know the worth of Golden Brown,
Not as a sign of cooking excellence
But monetary wisdom we have seen
That masters all the ills that man is heir to.
The Tory Blues bring icy chills to mind
And grunting, sweating, dreary lives for all
To make fat cats that puzzle every will.
We, therefore, must keep what we have right now
As we can see How 'ard life may be otherwise
When enterprises with great pitch and promise
Are made more muzzy by the thinking time
Becoming images and pipe-dream cons
That lead us to disaster in the end
And limit numbers of those to Let win.
The present way hoists up the flag of truth
That opens eyes to bright reality.
But soft you now! Let not the others know
The secret of success that Two Bs show.

The Daily News

Through the leaves and through the window
The sun makes dappled patterns on her dress;
The aged lady in her aged chair is almost hidden
By the broadsheet copiously printed over with
Irrelevances hoping to be news.
She reads intently. Impassioned concentration.
Determination to understand. Her interest quickens.
No doubt, the pressure in her arteries increases
With each page she turns. She is confused.
Cannot believe that actions so reported
Describe the real behaviour of Mankind.
The spectrum of behaviour can be vast –
Bestiality to sainthood is the range,
But looking at this present tranquil scene,
I do not know how much of living tumult she has had;
Perhaps she's reached a haven from distress,
Or never lived the stresses she now reads.
I only hope the lady in her pleasant little room
Can only see the pleasant things of life.
Her life seems cosy and well managed with frugality
That has been true salvation for the later years.
I said 'irrelevances'. How much that happens in the world,
How many tragedies and human suffering so read
Can have an impact on the reader's life?
There may be some: the price of milk; the buses are on strike;
The interest rates have changed; it's raining cats and dogs;
But there is nothing she can do about the words she reads
Without a mighty fuss. Fuss would take energy she has not got.
Or, who to go to? That takes thinking time.
The buying of a paper every day becomes a habit of robotic
    strength.
It's read, it's wondered at, it lets you paddle through to bedtime.

Then it is thrown away. Hurrah — it is recycled! And, guess what!
You buy its clone and read more words no more related to you
Than the lot before.
I watch the gracious lady as she turns the last page of
The broadsheet in her hands. She lets it fall, a crumpled heap,
Upon the floor. She takes her glasses from her face,
And lays them neatly on the arm of her best chair.
Her head droops forward and she floats into Elysium
And falls asleep.

The crumpled heap of all the worldly woes becomes a load of
    garbage.
In her life, the things more real to her remain the same.
The sun still watches through the window-pane,
And dances joyful frolics on her pretty dress;
It keeps her warm and cosy till the time comes round again for tea.

Festival Time

Rush to the water. Dive through the waves.
Scramble back out again, join the beach raves.
Barbecues blazing, the meat on the turn,
Make the cooks watch it before a big burn.
The music, some call it, is blaring away,
Cavorting guitarists are having their day.
The crowds are so dense that there's no room to dance,
They jig up and down and make little advance
In any direction – north, south, east or west.
The stifling heat and a sweaty string vest.
Cavorting to lose all the cares of their lives.
The way they behave means that everyone strives
To clutch at the straws that give flashes of fun,
But when it's all over, what have they all done?
The fear of the worst never comes into mind,
To think badly of them is very unkind.
Some fall by the wayside with penalty harsh
And others will always find life a vast marsh.
The perils are man-made in pills, jabs and drink;
Go over the limit, they're soon on the brink
Of dangerous practices, over the top,
When fatal results are too rapid to stop.

The thousands who go to a rave by the sea
Are outnumbered by those who feel equally free
To wallow in mud that is churned by their feet.
The music's the same and the barbecue meat.
The scene is more vast and the noise more sustained.
If you're right in the middle your neck must be craned
To have just a glimpse of the stars on the stage
With their hoarse-making songs and their bouts of mock rage.

The fans gently rock back and forth where they stand
Like a field full of wheat in a breeze that is bland.
Their arms spiral upwards and seem, at a glance,
To be beanshoots a-twirling and wanting to dance.
The roar of the clapping has crackerly sounds
Like a speeding jet fighter that's knowing no bounds.
The thumping of speakers seems part of a scheme
To create a winding and increasing stream
Of people with earache all screaming for aid.
The sun, then, decides that its light must now fade.
The music continues without interruption.
The litter increases to cause more corruption
Of areas meant for the overnight stay.
Find a spot for the tent in the very best way.
Now, deep in the darkness and late of the hour
The music on stage has been stopped and lost power.
A sprawling encampment is growing apace
The scramble's increasing to find a good place
To get undercover in case it may rain
And have time asleep. Then it starts all again;
But all through the night in the twinkling camp
Comes a scatter of noise as guitars try to vamp
The songs that have hammered the air all the day,
But those who are knackered will sleep anyway.
There will be a few who have drunk just too much
And their comings and goings will be thought to be such
That an unwanted guest may arrive or be sent
And be incoherent regarding intent.
Come wind or come rain, the next day will begin
With attempts to get litter to the handiest bin.
All eyes now prised open, the sun overhead,
A full English fry-up will stand in good stead
The fans who have stuck it and want much much more.
The whole surging mass of them move by the score
To get close as possible up to the stage.

The stars reappear with their songs and mock rage.
The loudspeakers thump as they did hours before
And it's more and it's more and it's more and it's more.
A frenzy of raving increases the sound
As cheering and screaming and laughing abound.
Enjoyment is everywhere clearly to see,
Elsewhere is not where all these people would be.
After three days of using their energy thus
They will have little left and will probably cuss
The thought of returning to everyday life;
But some may have trouble placating the wife.
The thousands who long to repeat it again
Will cherish the memories that they retain,
And an innermost glow will pervade through their mind
When looking at photographs, nice and unkind.
'Did he really do that? It's hard to believe';
'Good heavens, I thought she was much more naïve.'
It is 'hairdown' events when related to all
That will lift reputations or cause a downfall.
But many would join them, if only they could,
And hopefully doing no more than they should.
Let memory serve with a story to tell
That what you may fancy, in small bits, is swell
Too much of a good thing is bound to be bad
And too much loud music will send you quite mad.
So keep down the volume and stay fit and well,
Live long and be able to have tales to tell.

Man's Folly (Memoirs of a Casualty)

A soldier with a gun stood over me,
His uninvited bullet in my leg.
I looked into his eyes and tried to see
What mood was welling in his soul and mind;
Or were robotic diktats pushing him?
I had a different uniform to his,
So, logic showed, I was his enemy.
But men, beneath their clothes, are all the same.
I feared that he would fire another shot,
And, in a flash, destroy all life in me.
A millisecond of my worldly time
Used up by micro-movements in his hand
Would guillotine achievement that I had,
And slice my dreams, ambitions, future plans,
To make me be a certain nothingness.
I formed a nervous smile on my face
And raised my arms to show I had no gun.
His hesitation seemed a million years.
He put his gun down, pushed his helmet back
And propped me up against a broken wall.
He saw my pack and got a bandage out,
And, with a gentle touch, secured my wound.
We did not understand each other's talk.
As is a note of music clear to all,
He asked a question known to everyone
And said, in sympathetic tones: 'OK?'
He helped me to my feet and took me back
To where a hospital had been set up.
A surgeon got the metal out of me;
But rules of war made me a prisoner.
My foe turned friend began to talk with me,
And, as we slowly learned each other's tongue

We found that fighting did not make much sense.
I had not hurt a single soul myself,
But he was one up in the score of war
As his one shot at me had blooded him.
I had much thinking time ahead of me.
In taking stock, life was not all that bad,
Albeit, there were those who tried to leave.
For some strange reason, my philosophy
Persuaded me to stay just where I was.
Unbroken faith dictated victory.
However many years it took to win,
My side, without my help, did pull it off
Then from the battlefield and prison camp
We all streamed home to where our lives had been.
Oh what a change was there: no house, no town;
In many cases, too, no family.
A start from scratch faced everyone, at first.
There was assistance for material things
And many handouts from the public purse.
Great opportunities were opened up
To catch up with our studies and our skills,
But application was the tricky bit.
A good night's sleep devoid of memories
That shudder your whole being any time.

'My God! I've got a job at last,' but oh
It is the one my best friend would have had
If only he had lived to tell the tale.
I feel his ghost sits in the chair with me.
We work as one, more closely than before,
But worst of all, he comes to bed with me.
I see his suffering in high relief
As though the day had come again, once more,
When he was cut to pieces by my side.
The arguments for war are made quite plain.

Two words sum up the attitudes of 'SIDE'.
They are, of course, Aggression and Defence.
With everything that happens in this world
A simple formula applies to all:
Where Action is, Reaction will occur,
The last resort: inevitable fight
Displays the great flaw in the human gene.
With all the gifts of talk and reasoning
The mind goes blank, frustration takes the stage
And mayhem floods the scene and writes the script.
But when the show is over and the dust
Has settled, as it would after a storm,
The most that is achieved is to rebuild
And put things back to what they were before,
Or as you hope; but nothing that is hurt
Is ever quite the same, the scars will show
And live alongside all the victory.

I write this précis of my thoughts on war
Some sixty years beyond the real event,
But my indented memories are there
Although the edge is blunted from my rage.
A resurrection of those days came back
In circumstances that were quite bizarre,
For yesterday I went to see a film
Recalling incidents of fighting war.
I saw a clip that turned me icy cold,
I was not in it, but the feature shown
Was that same broken wall I leant against.
The next few seconds nearly stopped my heart.
A hand upon my shoulder from behind,
Pre-empted in a flash of mortal time
The sound of someone talking from the past

In English, tainted by a foreign tongue,
'How is ze leg? I hope it is OK.'
And there he was, my enemy-stroke-friend,
As old and time-worn as I am myself.

A tour of war is rarely worth the fare,
But if, from all the madness that is caused,
Belligerence can dovetail friendliness,
It is a plus that may have never been.
All people grow through many forming years
'So, catch 'em young.' The watchword of us all.
If those in charge can learn a different way,
A peaceful world may have a chance to stay.

Traffic-Light Dreams

Ten minutes of my working day is spent at traffic-lights.
I queue like all the others do determined for my rights,
But when I'm sitting thinking there, I get a little chance
To let my fantasies fly free and have a little dance.

Fantasy 1
I'd like to be a postman who would jumble up the mail.
I'd have such fun to watch the people following their tail
To find out anybody else who got their mail instead.
They'd all be so exhausted that they'd stagger back to bed.
Another thing I'd like to do to help the day go by
Is X-ray all the parcels so to have a sneaky spy,
Particularly Christmastime when lots of things abound
And grievous disappointment will be shown by those who've found
The sender does not know them quite as much as they would like
And given them a scooter when they'd rather have a bike.
But if I was this postman I would have to watch my back
And rightfully agree with 'THEM' to give to me the sack.
But, in the end of course, I'd have to give them their sack back.

Fantasy 2
I'd like to drive a railway train that never stops at all.
I'd whizz through all the stations, shutting ears to every call
To let the people off at this or that place on the way,
And going round the corners I would make the coaches sway.
For those who like a thrilling ride and get a kick from speed
I'll give them all they need to have to get their spirits freed.
Of course there'll be some frightened folk who think I'm off my
    head;
Maybe that they are right. There is a chance to end up dead.
I'd have to slam the brakes on, just to live another day.
I'm bound to get the sack, and well deserved in every way.

Fantasy 3
I'd like to fly an aeroplane up in the bright blue sky,
To loop the loop and twist and turn and swoop down by and by,
And make the people crane their necks to see me at my tricks.
I'd see them run for cover or I'd send them all for six.
The trouble is that those on board may be a bit confused,
I'd have to say, 'I'm sorry if you're getting slightly bruised.'
Then, up above the clouds we'd soar to get a better view
When gaps revealed the earth beneath a sky of azure blue.
I'd do a victory roll or two and give the wings a flick
But not too much, you understand, or some may feel quite sick.
Of course, I'd have to land sometime when fuel got too short,
And those on terra firma will not think I'm having sport.
If runways hit the wheels too hard there will be quite a jolt,
But when the wheels stop turning I'll jump out and quickly bolt.

Fantasy 4
I'd like to drive a motor coach down narrow country lanes,
But some would not agree with me and think I'd lost my brains.
Think, though, of what it would be like with hedges flying by
And animals all running scared and wishing they could fly.
The crossroads would be thrilling, like roulette from far-off Russia,
But if I met a harvester it may become a crusher.
On second thoughts it might be best to find a motorway
Where I could have my foot to floor and shout 'Heigh-Heigh,
    Heigh-Heigh'
And lanes run side by side and you can nip across them all.
An empty coach would be the best to instantly enthral
A farmer leaning on a fence or driver up ahead
To watch the way I weave about and see the way I sped
Right out of sight of all of them. Then like a shooting star.
That flashing light of azure blue upon a stripy car.

Fantasy 5

I'd like to be a captain on a mighty ship of war.
I'd blaze away like billy-o at everything I saw.
I'd race around in circles till the crew begged me to stop.
I'd fire anti-aircraft guns, I love to hear them pop.
Torpedoes would go everywhere and cause an awful mess.
The fun would be if aircraft came to put us in distress.
I'd put up flags all over in the hope that we are seen,
But someone, on the radio, might ask me what they mean.
I'd quite expect a mutiny or other kind of fuss,
I'd have to get ashore at night and try to catch a bus.

Fantasy 6

I'd like to drive a Grand-Prix car, positioned up at pole,
And when the red lights all went out I'd have to go, not stroll.
————————————!
This fantasy will have to wait. Reality has come.
I've got a sinking feeling in the bottom of my tum.
I am in pole-position and the red light has gone out,
But somebody is hooting and the others start to shout.
I must have been in dreamland and forgot just where I was.
It was a disappointment with reality because
The red light was the traffic-lights at crossroads into town.
But what a lovely time I had, although I was a clown.

J.C.

Poor Jesus Christ, he tried to do so well
To show his fellows how to keep from hell
His efforts were belittled at the top.
There was a chance his message may well flop.
But common sense in all that he had said
Convinced a few to follow him instead.
And so began a train of goodly thought
Passed on by the apostles truly wrought.
The vision that he had within his mind
Was simply to highlight those things 'unkind',
And change them round for everybody's sake
By letting in the light, and thereby, make
A brighter future with a peaceful mode.
But his clear thinking hit against the code
Established to give power to the few
Who relished telling stories, false or true,
About the need for ritual and troth
Depicting God a monster full of wrath
Unmerciful to those who kick the trace
And find themselves in conflict with God's grace.
Sweet Jesus preached forgiveness in all things.
Be kind to all: compassion without strings;
Give quarter where the instinct is to fight
To stay alive and beat aggressors' might.

Remember that he grew up as a Jew,
And was a faithful member, and he knew
The great potential of the learned cult
That could cast far and wide the big result
Of universal harmony and joy,
If only it would build and not destroy

A wider magnanimity to life
And have a view of God devoid of strife.
A loving God, a strong supporting hand
To help the weak, and always understand
The limitations of humanity,
And guide each one from their calamity.
A study of his start in life as man
Could not have been more low. A social ban,
Refused a place of birth within an inn,
But hidden in a stable with his kin.
The landlord disapproved of what he saw,
And was suspicious of the load she bore,
Considering that they had just been wed.
For this is plain from what St Matthew said.

The Star of Bethlehem is thought to be
A timely comet all had come to see.
The Jewish nation had for countless years
Yearned for a saviour to quell their fears
Of endless persecution by their foes,
Who came from all directions causing throes.
And now, with Herod's despotism rife,
A clutch at straws might give their legend life.
Within the crowd that saw the Star that night,
Were three men of distinction and great might
Who would be welcome into Herod's court,
And, with a little impishness, be bought
With whispers of a child's unusual birth
Within a cattle shed to show his worth.
These three wise men joined in the joke of it
To go to Herod and use cunning wit,
And storytelling of the utmost skill
That made a legend come to life, until
He really did believe that flesh and bone
Had come to oust him from his royal throne.

The desperate measures that he put in place
Caused panic and a life-preserving race
To save as many children on the way
By dashing to some country, there to stay,
Until the coast was clear: the tyrant dead,
And coming home had lost its biggest dread.

As Jesus grew and helped his father's trade,
Where useful things of carpentry were made,
He toiled as any boy, around that age,
To please his parents and to reach the stage
Of growing as a man of goodly tone
Fulfilling aspirations of his own.
This found him reading in the synagogue,
And, with awareness, formed a catalogue
Within his mind of how the elders missed
Compassion in the soul, and so dismissed
The essence of a goodly life for all.
For Jesus, this became a clarion call.
A full grown man, still never understood
By elder circles, turned to those who would.
He gathered round him men of his own kind
Who each could listen with uncluttered mind.
The saying that is heard down through the years
'A prophet, in his own land, wastes his tears.'
And so it was that Jesus and his band
Preached new humanity far from their land.
The great conviction that he could impart
Made people think that, from the very start,
They had a heavenly being close at hand
Who could make all their daily lives less bland.

He had the precious gift of giving peace,
Relieving stress and let poor souls release
The symptoms of their nervous aches and pains,
So that they felt recovered from their strains
And many other things they saw him do
Were classed as miracles and heaven-sent too.
With modern knowledge of the sciences
These happenings, with all our consciences,
Could not have been the way that they are written
However much a person's thoughts are bitten
By bugs of superstitious fantasy
That want to make things real from travesty.
At nowhere in the record that we read
Did Jesus claim, or even have the need
To have a supernatural gift at all.
'Our Father . . .' means that God is Dad to all.
If you believe in God or not it's plain
That Jesus proved an unsurpassing gain
To humankind in all recorded time
So, make conditions for receptive clime
And Christian teaching will grab shut-up minds
That struggle with their thoughts to lift the blinds
And let the light of common sense flood in
To guide their souls, forever, out of sin.

In spite of travel far and wide apace,
He knew the final task that he must face.
A space of three packed years for all of them,
And then full circle to Jerusalem
To make the final challenge to the group
Who would not listen and became a troop
Of thugs bent on a homicidal lust.
Destroying all new thought became a must.
To make his life worthwhile he must take
The biggest risk that any man can make

And meet his enemies, however strong,
Unarmed, but well supported by a throng
Of cheering, laughing, happy simple folk
Who hoped their Saviour would bad laws revoke.
But he knew what the outcome had to be
And, notwithstanding that, he had to see
If light would dawn and things might change at length.
His deep intelligence and mental strength
Knew that betrayal was the weakest link
Among his followers, pushed to the brink.
And so it was, as everybody knows,
The trial and the falsehood only shows
That, even now, redemption's hard to find
Among a people with a closed-up mind.

The irony in all this grisly scene
Is Pontius Pilate washing his hands clean
Of sending such an innocent good man
To be destroyed for doing good to MAN.
The crystal clarity of Jesus' mind,
His depth of knowledge of our humankind,
Not only baffled people of his age,
But always has caused awe at any stage
Down through the centuries of thinking time,
Because the faultless logic is sublime.
He was a man of genius, that's clear.
He needed no one from afar or near
To write his message to the universe,
But those who wrote of him were not so terse
With records, for they dressed the stories up
To heights of fantasy to form a cup
More palatable to the taste of men
Who relish fairytales, and hope that, then,
The hero of the story will become
Of greater strength than human, or that some

May even come to worship him at last
And turn a man into a god and cast
A spell of wizardry to grant their dreams.
But Jesus preached self-help and other themes.
His down-to-earth approach is still not seen.
It could be thought that he had never been
When things are undertaken in his name
That have their origins that are the same
As pagan rights before he did appear.
Stick to his teaching and we need no fear.
His message brings great benefits in store.
He was a unique man: we need no more.

Lonely?

You're never lonely if your life was full.
When all the people who you knew are dead,
You sift your memory and try to pull
The nicer ones, ignoring those you dread,
Into your fantasies without redress.
Although you cannot meet each one again,
You can enjoy 'best moments', and assess
The quality of all that you retain.
There will be places where good thoughts survive;
A meadow, lake or tree will bring to life
A scene of ecstasy, and so revive
A thousand details that are now more rife,
And in your grasp to taste the joy, once more,
Of touch and sound and scent upon the air.
A rainstorm can bring past events afore,
But it's more likely if the day is fair.
Look round your living space and let your eyes
Sear into every item that you own.
Get rid of anything that never tries
To smile right at you in a friendly tone.
The cosiness of all the things you love
Will replicate the never-ending joy
Of letting dreamland flutter like a dove,
Or the excitement of a brand-new toy.

Umbrella or Mushroom Cloud

Staring us all in the face
Is the ultimate choice by the human race.
Technical knowledge will soon
Arrive at a point of great joy or great gloom.
Nuclear physics is now
The Great Servant or Master for showing us how
Weather is kept as we like,
Or we make a device for the ultimate strike.
Rosy the future ahead
If we let nuclear power stand us in good stead.
Ironically true, although sad,
The same branch of science is horrendously bad.
Hope that world leaders will see
The choice is from two: they are Be or not Be.

Part Two

Spaciousness

Up, up into the air they went,
Until their precious fuel was spent.
The drag of gravity was weak,
So into orbit fast and sleek.
With all the junk that's up there now
It leaves you wondering just how
New orbiting devices fit
Into a path without a hit.
Discovery with risk is such,
Explorers cannot have too much
Excitement for the things unseen,
Or going where no one has been.
World records are obsessional,
But may end up processional.
So what! Someone has made their mark,
Although it may have been a lark.

Secret Night

The wrinkles in the bed showed what a night it was.
No 'snoozing calmly' could have left such twisted clothes.
The springs had had the hardest job of all, it seems.
The evidence of oscillations, to and fro,
But mostly up and down as well as round about,
Gave rise to images of breathless helter-skelter
To reach that peak of satisfaction at no risk
Of losing, just a minute part of energy
That had been harvested with ever-increased speed.
There was a whiff of great exhaustion in the air.
The windows were tight shut, which made the effort smell.
Where are they now who cast, for us, this lustful spell?
Perhaps it was not just an energetic game,
But creativity through focused thought
That makes the future species truly wrought.

A Bargain! Or is it?

'Buy one and you will get one free' –
The everlasting trader's plea.
'Buy two, the third is yours as well' –
The marketing has cast its spell.
'There's half as much more in the jar'.
'Thank heaven that we brought the car.
We'd never get it on the bus,
So there is no good cause to fuss.'
The offers come so thick and fast
That you must call a halt at last.
You stare down at the bulging trolley,
And suddenly you think of lolly.
'Can I afford this browsing game?
But, then, without it life is tame.
Oh look, those chops are really cheap,
If I don't take them I'll not sleep;
To think that chance has passed me by,
When I get home, I'm bound to cry.'

'But wait; what's in the fridge right now?
When we get home you tell me how
To stow these goodies till the time
Comes round for feasting: life sublime.'
When bargains deshelf all around
Another freezer may be sound.
Hang on, your house is fixed in size,
These freebies may not be a prize;
Perhaps a millstone round the neck,
So, quickly, quickly make a check
Of your real need for healthy guts
And dowse your urge to form more gluts.

The marketers want product flow;
They hope that you will never know
That offers are a man-trap too,
That make you feel he's begging you
For help to tussle with his peers,
But watch for crocodiles with tears.
Be happy, though, to shop at will.
So love what you're doing, unless or until
You sense that the 'bargain' you got was not real
As the discount suggests. Then, you'll probably feel
That the blips at the checkout are laughing at you,
As, in practical terms, one is better than two.

Emergency

Help is required by damaged mankind.
Hope for the ones that are rescued in time.
Thousands go under as their chance to find
Succour that never comes close to their clime.
Thought may be spared by the ones without stress.
Action, however, is needed to be
'Hands-on' for the victims to ease their distress.
Quagmire of living is fearful to see,
Once in the soft ground keep perfectly still,
Minuscule movement will make matters worse.
Another example of halting life's mill,
'Stop digging', your hole will soon damage your purse.
Hazards that people face every day
Come from a source that gives chance between two.
'Greed' comes the top of the jungle-life way,
Pushing out credible manners that woo
Stable relations and fairness, to stay
Always the norm. An Elysian dream,
Sadly, remaining a poetic theme.

Foresight

The thunderstorms of thought that flash the mind
Make reasoned arguments too hard to reach.
The memory that loses things is kind,
It is so vague it has no rules to breach.
Tranquillity of spirit can be gained,
And clarity of vision can be won
With mental processes that have been trained
To tackle all life's problems one by one.
When too much overlapping queers the pitch,
Much precious time, unravelling the threads,
Is used when eagle-eyeing which from which
Must be the way instead of knocking heads.
The need for tunnel vision may be clear,
But some peripheral consciousness must be
Sustained to keep alert in case of fear.
To be ahead will bring security.
Have wits about you; always watch your back.
Be nice to those you pass when going up,
And do not mock them for the skills they lack.
You flying past can be a bitter cup.
Keep deep within your soul the chance to fall,
And budget for a crash at any time.
Make sure you have some friends who are on call
To soften stumbles that are not a crime.
So play it straight, keep law upon your side,
And, if your pension fund is up to speed,
You'll have a goodly passage through life's ride;
But watch out all the time to judge your need.

The Changing Dream 1914–1918

They died to save the country that they knew,
But those who did survive saw that it grew
Into a strange society that flew
Straight at the face of things they thought were true.

The laces that held living ways as one
Were slashed. A liberated life was won,
With shorter skirts and Charleston, lots of fun,
New Oxford Bags and lying in the sun.

A new found order was embraced with glee,
But only those with money had a spree.
The wealth creators did not feel so free
When wages dropped at mines they could not flee.

As motoring became the latest craze,
Job losses, elsewhere, made the mood to blaze
And visions of a 'brave new world' did haze.
'All out' the cry that worsened living ways.

A tottering nation staggered into slump.
So many dreams descended with a bump,
And many hands of cards lost every trump.
The balls of fortune hitting every stump.

On sixteen years and things were looking up,
But bitter water fouled the nation's cup
As acid drops from storm clouds hailed a pup
Whose wolf-like greed took nations for its sup.

Some saw the storm clouds in the east,
But others would not recognise the beast
As it was planning an invasion feast
And started hurling down a warlike piste.

The ones who hung up arms, those years ago,
Were filled with trepidation, just to know
That those they fought before were still their foe.
Appeasement was the watchword: peaceful show.

And so it was that battle lines were drawn.
Some six years on the light began to dawn,
But, this time battle flags must all be torn
And talking must replace machismo brawn.

★   ★   ★

The Changing Dream 1939–1945

They died to save the country that they knew,
But those who did survive saw that it grew
Into a strange society that flew
Straight in the face of Churchill's famous 'Few'.

The finish of the rigours of the War
Meant people wanted more and more and more.
Designers changed the clothes that people wore,
But rations did not stop till fifty-four.

The sacrifice of men left labour gaps –
'I'll tell you what. We'll get some foreign chaps
To stop our tycoons getting into flaps.'
The nation was not asked. No hands gave claps.

Technology swept on at breakneck speed.
The world assumed insatiable greed.
The sixties came and human lust was freed.
The Flower People sowed no garden seed.

The new approach to life eroded codes
Of moral thinking and the 'old-time' modes
Designed to give stability and loads
Of risk-free living where real peace abodes.

The music scene sank in a mire of pop.
Mass media brought rubbish to the top,
Persuading all: 'There is no need to stop
Indulging basic instincts till you flop.'

The British Empire got a goodbye wave
To give all countries 'self-rule' that they crave,
But many did not think they were a slave
To the old Raj; 'To England, earn and save.'

So multiculturalism came to pass
In England where they found the greener grass.
Sometimes there will be tension in the glass
That shatters into bits reflecting class.

Transplanted trees don't always settle in.
Fighting the local climate's hard to win,
But global change will wear that theory thin
And all will merge and end up in the bin.

And, then, one day it will get sorted out
When all mankind abandons 'Scream and Shout'
And words will leave the dictionary like 'Lout'.
They'll wonder what the strife was all about.

They died to save the country that they knew.
The only thing unchanged was mother's stew,
But many chefs were forced into a flurry,
Because the people got a yen for curry.

The Soft Walk

The challenge in the mountains is the force of gravity.
The heights draw like a magnet, but magnetic earth pulls back.
The greater is the altitude you lose capacity.
It seems that you are heavier and want to lose your pack.
It is the lack of oxygen that makes the effort great.
Regrets will take a hold of you with every step you take.

This mountain stuff is not for me. Give me the lowly Downs
That roll across the southern scene beside the rolling sea.
No jagged rocks to stub the toes but softness underfoot
With tiny flowers and springy turf sweet scented with wild thyme.
The slopes are gentle and the paths are made to ease the climb.

Large forests, now, have grown where once the shepherds watched
    their flocks.
A relic of those pastoral days remains along the droves.
They are the dew-ponds set to catch the droplets from the mist
That often forms along the ridge whatever time of year;
The concrete rounds look up like eyes to catch the heavenly tear.

From Winchester to Beachy Head the undulating view
Unfolds itself with every step you take from east to west
Along the South Downs Way. Turn round and do it all again.
All aspects seen from east and west or north and south can be
A globe of relaxation from the vast tranquillity.

You're never far from sustenance, there's no need for a pack,
Unless you love alfresco on a lovely sunny day.
You get a sense of freedom as you walk for miles on end,
But there are some restrictions to give those some privacy
Who live amongst the downland as a way of life, you see.

111

The open space, the stretched-out views, the vastness of it all,
The upright cliffs of pure white that guard the pebble shore
Have beauty tinged with tragedy when used to end it all.
Behind the coast, down in the dales, where woodlands thickly grow,
There is a silence and a peace you have to feel to know.

Who are 'THEY'?

Who are 'They' who seem to know so much?
'They' say this and 'They' say that is true.
When you ask if 'They' are such and such,
You are held to shame if you pooh-pooh
That which has been globally assessed.
All is never doubted if 'They' say.
Truth of what 'They' say is not addressed.
Ghosts in the doubting mind cause some delay.
Then will the real facts come to light.
What 'They' Say, then, is rumours that are trite.

You Know!

'You know how it is,' he said a hundred times.
With every sentence he would end 'You know.'
But everyone he talked to did not have
The same experience he was telling of
So how could they respond to more 'You knows'.
A nod of understanding helps you out.
'Yer know, I think I will do that today.'
But you did not know till he told you so.
'I feel quite nervous at the thought, you know.'
The statement stands up on its own alone.
To complicate and emphasise the point,
Two words are added to the usual phrase:
'You know how it is, don't you.' How can you,
Unless you've had the same traumatic trip?
Without the 'You knows' all would be more clear.
Quite often he is asking for a tear,
More likely, it's a sympathetic ear.

Who Gets Punished?

There is no way to turn time back.
The action, now a part of history,
Was labelled, by the law, to be a crime.
The body started, straightaway, to rot.
A living body, now in custody,
Contained a thinking unit in its head
Which could not be arrested or contained.
The motive for a killing may be clear
To murderers, assassins and the like.
What of the contemplation time of years?
The memory remains. Are there regrets?
Lock up the body. Can we lock the mind?
A person's thoughts are their one privacy.
No way can any other person weigh
The good or bad intentions that don't show.
No measure can be put on scheming minds,
Which way they jump is anybody's guess.

The victims of a devastating crime
Have everlasting loss deep in their mind.
Whereas the criminal has had his fun,
He has lost nothing that he can't regain.
He bides his time and sees his sentence out,
And then is free to do his tricks again.
Apart from losing one they dearly love,
A family bears scars that never heal.
The amputation suffered by the group
Will cause a void impossible to fill.
The gyroscope of life is sent off course
And has to steer an unfamiliar route
Enforced by someone else's heinous crime.
The criminals are housed without a care.
The lives they upset: that's a grim affair.

Sort It!

You came here of your own free will.
It's grumble all the way with you.
Get out: why don't you go elsewhere?
You'll never find what you want here.
Why tarry in this dreadful place,
Depression never was so rife.
The sun shines brilliantly today,
Tomorrow clouds. What next?
The mood is full of discontent.
It need not be like this at all.
Let's penetrate the thinking fog
By talking, talking it all through.
Each one of us has points of view,
So find a table: put them on,
Pile up the ones that are alike.
Surprise, surprise, the ones then left
Are very few, you're best bereft.

Well?

The first use of the word 'WELL' is this:
To qualify the state of many things.
'Well done' will give a certain sense of bliss,
When 'Well connected' you can pull some strings.
'Well down the dip' is not good news for some.
'Well hung' can be interpreted at will.
'Well poised' may mean there's better news to come.
And so it goes with phrase on phrase until
The second meaning of the word is used.
'A well' is just a deep hole in the ground
To give a drink to those who don't get boozed.
So go 'well down' for water clarity.
You may strike oil, ending up 'well heeled'
And never needing acts of charity.
Go steady, though, to keep 'well in your field'.
The third, and strangest use of the word 'WELL',
Is as a 'stopgap', piece of time to think,
And has a bedfellow that goes 'Oh hell!'
'Well, let me see now, if I give the wink
To your suggestion. Well, I'm not too sure.
Well, give me just a day or two to see
If we can sort the scheme a little more.
Well, no, it isn't clear. Well, not to me!'
'Well, well' what is the sense of all of this?
To show convenience words that never miss.
But 'WELL' can start a hurtful question too
Like 'Well?! What has it got to do with you?'

Bright-eyes

Let all the stars give up the fight.
They have no power; they have no might
To dim the twinkle in your eyes
That straightway gives champagne goodbyes.
Light-headedness comes not from drink
But through my eyes that let me think
That what I see, but at a glance,
May give my eagerness a chance
To capture radiated glow
For longer than my right to know
The marvel that the world has seen
Comes from your windows that are green.

The Smile

A day in summer needs a cloudless sky
To keep our spirits on an active high,
But when you part your lips and show that smile
The seasons disappear and lose their style.
No element of climate can compete
With all the radiance that is complete
When you put sunshine in the deepest shade
And every part of feeling has been made.

Liz

There is a fine lady called Liz,
Who everyone knows as a whiz.
She gives of herself that's too much.
Her help towards others is such,
She hardly has time for a zizz.

Natasha

There is a sweet girl called Natasha,
Who we've always known as a smasher,
But thoughts in her mind
Put by people unkind
Will be beaten if she is a basher.

RICHARD GARRARD

KATIE . . . P.

Dear Katie . . . P., you're eighty-three,
A span of worldwide note.
If I write what you've done for me
A publisher would gloat.
May many more years come your way
For us to all hold dear.
Let's wish you have a lovely day
And have the same next year.

Pure Art

Is nothing more inert than blocks of stone?
Perhaps a sheet of paper, snowy white.
Creative minds breathe life into these things
To make an everlasting gem of Art.
With mallets, sharpened steel and heaven-sent skill
A graceful figure, or a portrait bust,
Erupts within the block to throw off chunks
And chips of stone to startle all the world.
A paper sheet receives the written word,
Or coloured medium to thrill the eye.
Imaginative minds give joy to all.
The ears and eyes contract as one to gloat
Upon dramatic scenes of fantasy.
Locked up, with many hundreds, in a box
The audience is totally transfixed,
And, in an hour or two of this confine,
Live different lives composed by someone else.
The show is over. Life, for real, comes back.
Serenity of Art is true enough.
It's coming back to living that is tough.

Start to Finish

Most people are extruded into life.
For others, doors are opened with a knife.
To live! To live! What happiness is there.
What joy to leave the bonds of being made,
To look such vastness in the eye at once.
Which way to go? Is that for destiny?
'First helplessness' means someone else's will
May mould what 'Starting-persons' may become.
Plod through the boggy land of daily school.
Extrude, once more, to join reality.
Feel free to make yourself the way you want,
Twist this and that way, laugh and cry at will,
Barge through the undergrowth of life,
Then look across the landscape of your deeds
And judge the failings up against success.
With eighty years or so upon the clock
Some inabilities will start to show.
Then must the final reckoning be made.
Possessions count for nothing in the end.
The lively ones can set their destiny
However much is written in a will.
The secondary share out is unknown.
So 'well created' living things depart.
All life will leave, the body will decay.
As everlasting as the turning earth,
More generations come to prove their worth.

The Challenge

What is all this living stuff about?
When can we be certain of the start?
How was time for living handed out?
Endless thinking minds are not that smart.
Queues of theologians, down the years,
Dreamt up stories to placate the soul,
Made some doubtful logic-killing fears,
Drew a mental picture of hot coal
Damning all the sinners to a hell.
Those who toed the line would get rewards.
All was made to cast a magic spell,
Giving the inventors power towards
Total domination of mass thought,
Setting up the image of Divine,
Fanning superstition till we've bought
Faiths that are opposed and don't entwine.
Hell with heaven makes a chain to bind;
Cast off any thought of having gods.
Make your heaven in another's mind;
Hell will be when everything's at odds.
Memory of you is all that counts.
Commonsense behaviour is the key,
Freeing living in controlled amounts,
Giving you command of liberty.
Wisdom is a time-acquired art
Delve history and learn from it by heart.

The Thief of Time

'Wait until the time is right!'
What a stupid thing to say.
Many people miss a chance,
Pushing kismet down their way.
World events will lead the dance,
Nature also joins the fray
With control of time's advance
Never changing day by day.
Fences used as thinking stools
Rot unseen in wasted time.
Many chances lost by fools
Vaporise without a rhyme,
Reason or the mental tools
Needed for a life sublime.
Stark reality that cools
Dawns a level-headed clime.
Waiting till the time is right
Causes chance to fade from sight.

Gratitude

Thank you for you being you.
There's never a sign
Of your spirit's decline
That would leave an intelligence gap.
You so look the part
That would break every heart
By setting a simple man-trap.
To make your heart warm
All must weather the storm
Of eruptions that few people crave.
It is 'stiff upper lip'
For this perilous trip,
Or someone will end up a slave.
The breakthrough was great
To have reached such a state
Of emotional bonding for good.
No words could express
The relief from all stress
That being with you ever would.
With gratitude joining up two
Both will whisper a 'thank you' for you being you.

'If Music . . .!'

Vibrating strings beneath the sawing bow
Sing out sweet sounds that thrill the eager ear,
Floating on air to let the people know
How little, in true music, brings on fear.
The trumpet, with its clarion call for all
Will herald more concordance of the sound
That spells its message by its rise and fall.
Crescendos and fortissimos abound
To make the strongest message of the score.
Then will diminuendo take the stage,
And presto spars with largo to give more
Dimension to the orchestrated cage.
The levitated harmony is such
That no one can deny they've been transfixed,
Or testify they've ever had too much.
The hope is that their views are clear, not mixed.
Old Masters stay the course, time and again,
There's something in their work that gives a lift
To spirits that are suffering life's strain.
But do not shut your mind to music's rift.

Now flip the coin and see the other side:
This branch of music, ringing in your ears,
Will need athletic prowess in your stride;
It calls for stamina and young in years.
Cacophony of sound, it seems to be,
But untold fans don't want the vibes to stop;
They want the beat to last eternally.
This widespread music-scene, described as pop,
Is when guitars compete with tribal drums
And microphones are bellowed at, ad lib,
With words all lost among the rum-atums
That no one could conceive as being glib.

The other forms of music as they're called,
Are as diverse as is a point-of-view.
Fans live in mental gardens that are walled,
But future sounds come musically new.

And so. If music is the food you love
To feed and nourish sentiments you treasure,
It lets your spirits flutter like a dove
Up to the heavens, giving endless pleasure.

A Story in Rhyme

This is a tale that a man lived to tell,
How he ended his life under some kind of spell.

Our Tom was a man of financial success.
His house was enormous, his garden supreme.
His social life frantic. He knew how to dress.
He knew all his workforce; they worked as a team.
His beautiful children were his pride and joy,
They wanted for nothing, and put to good use
The massive resources that he could deploy.
Though some things that happened were classed as abuse.
His plan, for the long-term, was dynasty-led:
The eldest son, Thomas the Second, would be
The rightful successor. No more need be said.
But time is a moulder of things, don't you see.
As calendars came and calendars went
And siblings of Tom-two got wind of his tricks
They thought that his actions put out the wrong scent.
So all of them gave to their lives a new fix.

Tom-one had been grooming Tom-two for his job
To get him to learn all the skills of the age
For greatest return that may make him a nob.
The watchword was 'Keep to the law at each stage.'
But Tom's other children developed their way
Of thinking out living beyond Old Tom's realm.
Their spouses and partners were having their say,
Which put out strong vibes to the hand on the helm.
To jump a few decades and come to the time
When Tom-one should give to Tom-two his real chance
To prove that his training allowed him to climb
The stairs to the boardroom and dance the sweet dance

Of success and achievement of ultimate power.
He'd reckoned on vertigo, way at the top –
To be up so high would make anyone cower;
A false step would cause a chaotic long drop.

The second in line was a fellow called Fred.
He struck out away from the family firm
And got himself trained as a doctor instead.
'Twas 'business for profit' that caused him to squirm.
The third place was held by a sister called May
Who went down the medical road as a nurse;
The high life of leisure just drove her away,
Though her chosen career did not top up her purse.
Of all the four children who made up the set
Just one stayed at home, in traditional mode,
The daughter who lingered and never quite met
Her dream-man to fit her immaculate code.
Poor Patsy would seem to lose one for another,
Immersing her effort in bountiful things,
As well as a prop to her father and mother,
And having a lifestyle without any strings.

Tom-one was quite certain that things were OK.
Tom-two was acquiring business galore,
And everything flourished, in his kind of way.
But some aspects differed from what went before.
Suffice it to say that the Law got a whiff
Of something quite fishy regarding some chips.
Tom-two found his job at the edge of a cliff,
His gambling debts would have sunk many ships.
As the reckoning day began looming in sight,
An army of bailiffs were forming to strike.
Old Tom got to hear of the firm's pending plight,
And straightaway told Tom-two 'To get on his bike'.
So, back in the saddle for ageing Old Tom;

To grab at the reins and change gallop to trot.
Then trot to a standstill to miss a vast bomb
Of financial mess that would blow up the lot.
His knowledge of dressage then came into play
To order the steed to take many steps back,
And take a new route in a side-stepping way,
Then firm up control that Tom-two seemed to lack.

Morale in the workforce was boosted at once
When news of stability reached the shop-floor,
As Old Tom soon showed that he was not a dunce
By the way that he stopped Thomas-two, any more,
Diverting firm's assets to cover his debts,
And left him to sort out his financial mess
With step number one: 'Don't place any more bets.'
All hoped this would stop any more family stress.
The dreams of Old Tom dated back to his teens –
To gain satisfaction in all walks of life,
And never be classed with the crowd of has-beens,
He'd found, by the hard way, that living was strife;
But living things last but a very short span.
They showed much resistance, but stored up the cost
Of stresses and strains self-created by man
And so it turned out that ambitions were lost.

This tale now reveals that a longing for fame
Is bad for your health if you don't bear in mind
The spin-off on others is not quite the same,
And comeback in vibes can be very unkind.
The family crosswinds were taking their toll
As Old Tom's wife Martha was starting to fade.
She could not continue to fulfil her role
Of propping the household the way it is made.

She fought the good fight through the moods of her kin,
For she was the force that made Tom a tycoon,
Determined to make him be famous and win
A place in the annals: the ultimate boon.

But Martha and Tom were approaching the stage
When retirement beckoned. They had to slow down
And take a good look at their personal age,
A process unstoppable, crown or no crown.
The overworked tissues began to give way.
Poor Martha was first to need medical care,
Her stroke made her hospitalised for a stay
That caused all the family mounting despair.
The plus side was how they all gathered around
To give help to Old Tom's emotional fix
Which made sins of Young Tom be mentally drowned
With news of release from his financial mix.

While waiting for bulletins, hospital-wise,
Old Tom would gain comfort, when given the time,
By taking a chair, to his household's surprise,
And sitting for hours beneath a great lime.
This tree he'd first planted the week they moved in;
The sapling became the most dominant tree
And stood as a gauge of how life's web can spin;
Its shade gave illusions of being world-free.
The garden's main feature was marble and stone,
A circular fountain with multiple jets
Of water cascading with babbling tone.
The green on the stone was from water it wets.
Some added attractions were sculptures to show
An artistic liking for bodily form
Depicting a woman exuding a glow
Of mystical happiness meaning to warm

The hearts of beholders to bring them great joy
As two little children, she held in her arms,
Were, both, clinging tightly to their special toy.
The concept was soothing and readily charms.

A hospital all-clear, and Martha was home,
But frail and not quite the old stalwart she was,
So gone were the days when she supervised loam
Being spread on her garden for prize blooms, because
She sponsored the annual colourful fete . . .
But Joseph, the gardener, knew what to do –
The whole thing was right if he rose to the bait
Of winning some cups and a wage increase too.

Just pause for a little. Consider the scene.
The years have so rushed beneath everyone's feet
That Old Tom and Martha were having to glean
The comforting memories making life neat.
Some fifty years on from the day they were married,
They knew it was time, now, to update their wills,
To look back: get sight of the time they had tarried
And focus their thoughts upon possible ills.
The shadow that loomed was the health of dear Martha.
With everything done in prolonging her life,
Old Tom lost his craving for business, but rather
Kept brooding on living a life without wife.
The others were happy with things as they were,
All shutting their minds to their possible fate;
But health-weather changes quite quickly from fair
To be a vast sudden and terrible spate.

It had been a habit, on nice sunny days,
To sit on the terrace, as teatime came round,
And plan out the next day in various ways.
The fountain: the only extraneous sound.

Young Lucy, the parlour-maid, set out the meal
With sandwiches having traditional fill.
The chatter was endless and made them all feel
That life was eternally happy, until
The instinct of May told her something was wrong.
Old Tom had dozed off in his favourite chair,
But May knew her mother was not very strong
And seemed very silent although sitting there.
The others were signalled to keep very still
To allow sister May to confirm her worst fears.
Dear Martha had left them whilst they took their fill,
But now, joyous teatime was dampened by tears.
The greatest dilemma was telling their dad.
He had to be woken before medics came.
His instant reaction was sure to be bad,
And keeping him calm was the ultimate aim.
He was very old, but surprisingly well
And showed no emotional shock when he knew.
He'd faced many crises, and willing to tell
The best way to go is a practical view.

When all the funereal process was done,
Old Tom and his daughter had much to decide.
Inheritance: what are the things to be won?
The possible interests were bound to collide.
But Patsy had not wasted time, living home,
She'd studied and gained a diploma or two
In financial know-how while writing a tome
To help small investors who wanted to woo
The stock market dealers who give good returns
From modest investments to help in old age
And save all the fingers from serious burns.
So Patsy, with knowledge, came good at this stage.
All Martha's possessions were willed to Old Tom,
Which meant that no share-out would come till he died.

The family met and, with legal aplomb,
Made Patsy the spokesperson who specified
A suitable trust to avoid too much tax
By passing the house and its treasures within
To family members, behind no one's backs
With upfront clear mandate so each one will win.
This gave Tom and Patsy the chance to reside
With residents' rights for as long as they wish.
The trustees appointed would have to decide
On sharing the goodies down to the last dish.

The years trickled by at the same speed as ever.
The old man got frailer and had a bad knee,
His big fear was such that his frailty may never
Allow him to sit by his favourite tree.
From there he could gaze at his garden and fountain.
The rippling water would send him to sleep.
His dreams would transpose a small hill to a mountain.
He'd doze and try hard to remember the past
And sift out the bits that gave him the most pain.
As time came for him to go in he would cast
A glance at the fountain and hope that, again,
His strength would allow him to see it once more.
The next day had overcast weather and wet,
In fact, for a week, the rain tended to pour.
His last great ambition was: go where he met
The light of his life and only true friend.
To get there would seem to create too much stress.
So, left with his thoughts, that he tried to subtend,
He focused his vibes to give little distress.

The fountain had come uppermost in his mind –
It gave him a symbol of family bliss:
The water, the statues in which he could find
The tranquil sensations that most people miss.

A lovely day dawned and he called upon May
To help him to get to his seat by the lime.
The weather was warm and he wanted to stay
As long as he could, irrespective of time.
He dozed off a little, but never quite slept.
His vision was failing and tended to see
Real people, in shadows and sunlight, who leapt
Up from the fountain, all laughing with glee.
He strained to see whether he knew who they were,
And howled with frustration as nothing was clear.
Then, suddenly, he became fully aware
In his mind that the statue was showing some fear.
He visualised movement and got from his chair.
New life was within him and, lurching along,
He climbed on the fountain with barely a care
And clung to the statue, his heart full of song.
Dear Martha had come, so he thought, to take him
Away from his loneliness: leave all behind
The trappings of wealth. All the glory was dim.
At last he may float into realms that are kind.
His strength was now fading, his hold nearly done,
His upright position was starting to fold,
To all useful purpose his race was now won.

His slide to the depths where the water was cold
Was spotted by Patsy who raced to his aid.
He told her his thoughts with his ultimate breath.
And spelled out the good and the bad deals he'd made.
The story now ends as he fades into death.

New Horizons

With uni in the frame
Life won't be quite the same;
With lectures made to tease
And essays meant to please.
A train of thought may stop
When hunger makes you shop,
But soon you'll get it fixed
When you know how it's mixed
To give a working whole
And get a glowing soul.
Your sun is on the rise,
The world will be your prize.
When all the work is done
Real status will be won.

The Mobile Phone

The little box of tricks we call a phone
Is not the one our forebears used to know.
It is completely new and not a clone.
A quite unfettered nature it will show.
The digits in the number are eleven.
It takes as many days and nights to learn,
But when you've got the hang of it it's heaven
To bother all your friends at every turn.
How many little beasties always hide
Right at the bottom of a crowded bag?
Then, when it's found the ringing brat has died
Which makes your hope of chat begin to flag.

The mobile phone is everybody's need.
It is, no more, a novel bit of kit.
With texts you have to re-learn how to read.
A real Pied Piper's role you'll seem to fit
If your Call-sign gives welcome sounds to all
Who think the ice-cream man is on the way.
But what a joy to give a friend a call
To anywhere from anywhere, and stay
Upon the spot you first got the idea
Of telling them, without the use of wire,
Your feeling for them that you hold so dear,
And happy times with them that never tire.

Tardiness

Tomorrow and tomorrow, it is always jam tomorrow –
It's promises, all promises, in other words 'maybe'.
But promises are fragile and they often bring great sorrow.
Tomorrow is elastic. It's a never-ending plea.
It's always done tomorrow, if there is the time to spare.
Tomorrow-things need thinking-time and courage in the soul.
They always seem distasteful, and can give the heart a scare,
But bite the bullet, get it done, and score the winning goal.
Today will bring reality, achievement without doubt.
Don't give the jam the time to grow a furry coat of mould,
And put the 'put-off syndrome' most decidedly to rout.
Then make all good intentions gathered in against the cold –
The inner warmth from doing things spontaneously brave
Will give a full and happy life to know the time you save.

Reality

Howl out for reality in all the things that are.
Truth in sight and truth in sound and truth in every touch.
Strain out all impurities that dull the thinking star.
Weed out all the doubtful thought that's overgrown too much.
Bring to focus images of crystal clarity.
Thus will minds be purged of dross injected to distract,
Born of other's politics of doubtful parity.
Now can new horizons have a clearer view to act
Full of hope and prospect based on simple common sense,
Banning all the fairy tales that cluttered minds so far,
Giving true expression in a world that is not tense.
Howl out for reality in all the things that are.

Manias

The drumming wind, the lashing rain,
The earthquakes and the slide,
The heaving sea, the tragic main
Give life a risky ride.
Fly to a crevice in the ground
To save the fragile frame.
When safety seems to have been found
Just wait. The world will tame;
The isobars will part again,
The sun will give its rays;
A warming back relieves the pain
And heralds happy days.

The fear of atmospheric noise
Has always troubled men,
And women, sometimes, lose their poise
When storms invade their ken.
It's little wonder, years ago,
That lightning flash was Lord;
That sunshine brought the people low
In praise to help the sword.
A god was made for everything
That worried human minds
To shield the psyche from the sting
Of life as it unwinds.
The cult of 'one true god for all'
Advanced religious thought,
But, still, divisions made that fall
When global power was sought.
No single culture for mankind
Will ever be achieved
While superstition lets man find
Relief in tales he's weaved.

The psyche of the human brain
Can only spell disaster
When used on others to obtain
A skim of 'falsehood' plaster
To hide the truth, which is so dull,
When it is seen for real.
All stress would go if man could cull
His main Achilles heel.

Good common sense. What sense is that?
Does logic figure there?
Analysis should shed the fat
And show the truth that's bare.
A common way of seeing things
Without opinion's nudge
Would be a perfect state that brings
A walk without the trudge.
How many neighbours can you love
If they won't love you back?
The folklore 'hope for help above'
Depresses by its lack.
Philosophers, down through the years,
Some linked with the Divine,
Have always preached 'No need for tears'
If life and God combine;
And, then, when nature takes a hand
The god, which ever one,
Has followers who make a stand:
His work is being done.
Despair comes not to those in faith,
But to those standing by
With logic, not a man-made wraith,
As, in their efforts try
To show the scientific way
That governs life on earth,

And hope and hope that one fair day
Their message will have worth.
The reason for the world and us
Is never to be found.
So many theories miss the bus,
However that may sound.
Creationism has held sway
From Genesis till now.
Intelligent Design may play
A part to tell us how
The galaxy became, you see
And whether it will wreck.
There cannot be eternity,
Our world is but a speck
Of dust within the universe.
We need not know quite why.
It causes views that are adverse.
Let sleeping dogs just lie.

What is it all about?
A question veiled in doubt.
But anyone who thinks they're right
Will push the others out of sight.

Limericks

Two seagulls were flying up high,
One said, 'There's a new car I spy –
The windscreen is clear,
I can't fix it from here,
So I'll swoop down and score a bullseye.'

★ ★ ★

A driver was reaching the stage
Of feeling boxed up in a cage.
He swore at a truck,
But he had the good luck
To have coined a new phrase called 'Road Rage.'

★ ★ ★

A stable lad said to his mucker,
'I've been made to look like a sucker.
My wife has gone off
With a Polo Club toff.'
'You've got only one choice, you must chuck her.'

★ ★ ★

There was a man known as a 'larker'
His lifestyle could not have been starker,
But finding out more
Than he should, from next door,
Had earned him the nickname of 'Parker'.

★ ★ ★

145

A Christmas-store girl was a stacker,
And every one there was her backer.
They voted her best
In a beauty contest.
From a stacker she changed to a 'cracker'.

★ ★ ★

A sausage embedded in batter,
In excess, will make you much fatter.
Its colloquial name
Gives amphibians fame,
But, to toads, it is no way to flatter.

★ ★ ★

A fish that is known as a trout
Has a status that no one would flout,
But some who do eat 'em
Are old and beneath 'em,
And meddlesome, female and stout.

★ ★ ★

A cut off a bullock won praise
From a king in a mood to amaze.
The French word *surlonge*
Was made English: sirloin,
And a knighthood bestowed as a craze.

★ ★ ★

A US car boot is a trunk.
A bonnet a hood, or you're sunk.
In a jumble of words
That may make us all nerds,
Stay English and leave out the bunk.

★ ★ ★

A beautiful tree is a sight,
A valuable shade from the light.
If it spoke of the years
Full of laughter and tears
It would spread unknown species of blight.

★ ★ ★

Dear Larry 'O' worked out a ploy
To thwart Stanislavsky's main toy –
When the actor gets in
To the character's skin,
'Just try a little acting, dear boy.'

★ ★ ★

A postman was plying his trade.
He tried to count footsteps he'd made.
He said 'That is that'
When his arches went flat,
And his walk was like Chaplin, quite splayed.

★ ★ ★

A mathematician who fears
Imparting his tricks will bring tears
Should be quite resolved
Not to get too involved
With a bribe of a crate full of beers.

★ ★ ★

The captain said, 'Go up aloft'
As the last bit of rum he had quaffed.
I climbed up the mast,
My whole life went past
As the deck did not look very soft.

★ ★ ★

Why worry about the expense.
Get down to your very last pence.
The sky won't fall in,
Put your bills in the bin.
But, of course, this will never make sense.

★ ★ ★

Some people are mad about cricket.
The fans think the game is the ticket.
A batsman goes in
And it's great when they win,
But the footballers tell them to stick it.

★ ★ ★

A rugby match majors in sports.
It's speedy, and risky of sorts.
They roll in the mud,
Hit the ground with a thud,
And lucky if they keep their shorts.

★　★　★

A frog does not mind being soaked.
He's happy if he is not poked.
But crossing the road
He may see a flat toad
Who has met a car wheel and been croaked.

★　★　★

When rabbits dig deep in the ground
They hope they will never be found.
The fox's dream meal
Is more image than real
When his ears get the sound of a hound.

★　★　★

The theory of getting to sleep
Is the counting of hundreds of sheep.
If you count the last lamb
You're in quite a jam,
For what's left will be sticky and deep.

★　★　★

If you're young and are smoking a fag,
You may think you're some sort of wag.
If you're quizzed by a cop
The shop may get the chop
When you let the cat out of the bag.

★ ★ ★

Whatever's the matter with Joe,
His actions are languid and slow.
He's had a rough day,
I have sworn not to say
How the gaff could, most certainly, blow.

★ ★ ★

The sunset is full of romance.
It brings on a slow dreamy dance.
The light will then fade
And a statement is made:
'Down, Rover, you haven't a chance.'

★ ★ ★

What time will the next train arrive?
The timetable does not contrive
To make me believe
If it stops, it will leave?
Whilst the most of us are still alive.

★ ★ ★

Now sing all the songs that you know,
And bellow them out high and low.
Your neighbours may say
You're for showbiz one day
But, at present, please pack up and go.

★ ★ ★

When things look remarkably bleak,
And pressure makes you nearly shriek,
Think of blessings you own
Above those all alone
Who are paddleless all up the creek.

★ ★ ★

There was a young fellow called Jim
Who burgled our house on a whim.
He confronted the wife.
Result: trouble and strife.
Remorse came, quite quickly, to him.

★ ★ ★

I met a big dog in the park.
I knew that my chances were stark.
His look let me know
That he wanted to show
That his bite was far worse than his bark.

★ ★ ★

151

The singers are more than the song,
As many can make it sound wrong.
Auditions are hell
And many will tell,
'You're far from an angelic throng.'

★ ★ ★

I was feeding a horse with some hay
On a beautiful summery day.
I said, 'Right for a ride?'
But the horse soon replied
With a snort and an emphatic 'NAY'

★ ★ ★

The parson was setting the scene
To help people's lives to be clean.
He saw someone there
Who gave him a scare.
As he'd been where he should not have been.

★ ★ ★

There was a young fellow called Kelly
Who said he knew all about telly.
Repairing a set,
The wires he met
Made him trip and end up on his belly.

★ ★ ★

Two gossips were having their tea.
'. . . there's no sense of fashion you see.
The hat was a mess.
But, as for the dress . . .'
'You rotten old hag, that was me.'

★ ★ ★

When Taffy was drinking with Paddy
They met, in the bar; the wee laddy
He wanted a round,
Not in drink, I'll be bound,
But the others would act as his caddy.

Of a Day – Mark 1

As I prise up my eyelids for the dawn,
My eyes pass messages of hope and dread.
I wonder which card, from the pack, I've drawn
To give a chance of earning daily bread.
The minefield hazards facing all each day
Disturb the peace of mind, creating fear.
A straight and well-lit path is all we pray,
Perhaps a day, good luck if it's a year.
The years race by, I audit what I've done;
It's doubtful if the details come to mind.
How many situations have I won?
The lost ones may be difficult to find.
Just meditate upon the good I did,
And highlight good that others did for me.
A helping hand is rare to have amid
Life's thickets as we wrestle to be free.
When twilight comes to finish waking hours,
The day I've had may give an aching head,
So then, like every other one who cowers,
I, stealthily, creep up the stairs to bed
To be cocooned where only faces show
The glow of peace: I do not give a damn.
My eye-borne signals: I don't want to know.
My eyelids drop, I almost hear the slam.
The next day is so very far away,
I may indulge in fantasies . . . or pray.

Of a Day – Mark 2

As I flip up my eyelids for the dawn
My eyes will sparkle at the sight of day.
Anticipation at the card I've drawn
Is most exciting for my work and play.
The thrill of doing what I most enjoy
And being paid for it: a dream come true.
Opposing forces meet a cunning ploy.
I always show I see their viewpoint too,
Which calms the waters; lets me do my thing.
Before they get their breath my thing is done,
And so disguised that they think they can sing
Of triumph by the clever way they've won.
With working done and satisfaction gained,
It's entertainment time to play some game –
A lively game that keeps the body trained.
And then, with hope the next day is the same,
I, happily, stroll up the stairs to bed
To be cocooned where only faces show
The glow of peace: I'm grateful to be me.
My eyes decide there's nothing I need know.
My eyelids slowly close to set me free.
The next day is not very far away,
But I've got time to fantasise . . . or pray.

Part 3

Progressive World

Into the world, one instinct: food.
A screaming mass of tissue has arrived.
What will 'IT' do to lead the world?
It has two decades to present itself.
The window on the world is vast.
'No Knowledge' is a fertile field
For outside influence galore.
But time to look this way and that,
Then fix a laser eye on life
And find an ever-growing way.
An endless crowd of gurus mould the mind
Like sculptors who will chip away the dross.
This educated, full of life, result
May fix life's focus on a single theme
And target fairways never trod before.
Inventors have the greatest gift of all –
To shine a light where darkness reigned supreme.
But, ups and downs will pave a rugged path,
With tunnel light at two per cent at first.
Tenacity, self-faith will win reward.
So, make it work: apply the greatest will.
Squeeze out the effort, exude vibrant life.
Stretch out the sinew and the muscle mind.
It's bound to give results.

The whiz-kids swim against the flow.
Unique inventions always bring a scoff.
They unseat what is thought to be the truth.
Use flaming vision to dispel the fog.

Keep on, keep on, momentum must not flag.
The final trick with every good idea:
'Development to monetary gain.'
Be secret: patent every tiny jot.
Block out the ever chance of piracy.
A good idea will market on its own,
If managed in a knowledgeable way;
And, with success, each dog will have its day.

The World Goes Round

Along the road to meet their fate
A mass of humans sprawl.
The leaders will anticipate
But many hardly crawl.
A glacier of saline cells
That grinds a groove through life.
Cacophony of views and spells
And manufactured strife.
Will nothing ever sort this out?
It's carved so deep in rock,
Acceptance has built-in distress
For those who have no stock.
How can one person show success?
Technology needs teams
Of equal strength and doggedness
To satisfy the dreams.
When I drop off the glacier
I hope the sea is calm
And things may be much glassier
If I have done no harm.

RICHARD GARRARD

Childhood: Or is it?

With children in the meadow and an azure cloudless sky,
A picture conjured up to calm the mind . . .
A country life was always thought as an idyllic high,
Escape from grubby towns of every kind.
Illusions such as this were lost to vision long ago,
Computers reign behind each cottage door.
The children find the meadow just another window bore
In flashes as they change their video game.
Their bodies, like excited dogs, would love to run and jump,
Robotic thrills make all that very tame.
Incredulous green living goes, with rubbish, to the dump.
Their eating is a way to cram the gut,
To take the mind off hunger and ignoring how they're fit.
Be 'with it' or they end up in a rut.
But does this endless viewing put an edge upon their wit?

The Cruise

The ship, the cabin, entertainment and the food.
A mass of people who are quite unknown.
A fresh new life fixed in a frame of time.
A passage booked a year or more ahead.
A lottery against the health you have to keep,
Until the time the gangways are withdrawn.

The ship is free to sail the seven seas, but wait.
This venture is a bus run for the crew.
Wherever they are going they have been before.
Their task: to make it happy and relaxed,
So that the punters come in thousands year on year.
This titan package, on the rolling sea
Has made its mark in modern history.

The Old Salt

He sits there like a figurehead,
The old man on the quay.
The seagulls know how he was bred,
That stalwart of the sea.
Like all, his eyes see waterscape
Whose moods can be unkind,
But life has left him no escape
From thoughts that he can find
Beneath the water blanket where
The past of man is deep.
He knows the tragic rubbish there
That caused the world to weep.
However much technology
Is used to ride the waves,
The fight with man's ecology
Still leaves his kind as slaves
To raging storms and heaving swell
That toy with all that floats
To give the seaman merry hell.
The seaside sits and gloats;
Its breaking waves foam at the mouth
Of every hungry shore
That's facing north, east, west or south,
Delighted to have more
And masticate with rocky teeth
To swallow without trace
And hide destruction way beneath
That terrifying place.
But then, the old man on the quay
Can tell of better days.
The scene is pure tranquillity
As most would like always.

The mirrored sky of blue is there.
The seaside comes alive
With minimum of clothes they wear
Who crowd there and contrive
To get the sun to grill them brown,
Improving how they look,
But, sad to say, they're laying down
Deep trouble as they brook
The scorching sun, with unseen rays
That penetrate so deep
It will not be for many days
That skin will start to creep.

A day of joy beside the sea,
With frolics in the waves,
Or raise a sail and there will be
What every seaman craves,
To skim across that water plane,
Forget what is below
And let the canvas take the strain,
Whichever way you go.
For many it's a gorging time
To eat the things they shouldn't
Or get caught up in petty crime
When, normally, they wouldn't.

The seasons change before his eyes,
That mariner of old,
But steadfast by eternal ties,
Impervious to cold,
Completely weatherproof is he
That fund of knowledge on the quay.

Precious Metal

To throw and lift and row and jump and run,
It all looks easy and a lot of fun.
The aim is to defeat whoever's there,
But make the whole thing desperately fair.
Olympians are such a special lot.
To take part means you've given your best shot.
A place on podium is glory won,
It shows to all your moment in the sun;
But dedication and tenacity
Is anything but sweet simplicity.
The training to perfection is not seen,
In many cases dogged by 'might have been'.
Complete immersion in the sweat and tears
Will hone the body to withstand the fears
Of failure to achieve the dearest aim
And clear the pitch of any sense of shame.
The pinnacles of sport are there to grab
If you can discipline your body flab.

Fangs

The grasses of the world are full of snakes.
Go tiptoe through the meadowlands of life.
Achilles heels are nearest to the bites
That lurk among the sweetness growing there.
The venom carriers that slither by
Can be identified by fork-tipped tongues,
Or by the rattle heard from wags with tales
Who play a hollow sound that has no tune.
A discord that will jam the ears with lies
And cross-talk seeming very like the truth.
Constrictors try to tie up fatal knots.
The jaws of complicated jargon stretch
To vast proportions to devour the prey
Of 'bargains' disappearing without a trace,
For, having feasted on the trusting fool,
The Master Snakes might vanish with the wind.
Strike first: make them be ultimately skinned.

Life of Virtual Ecstasy

The slogan for the world might be 'Fix everything with love.'
The symbol of a peaceful world has always been the dove.
The loving of a neighbour must be clearly understood,
As two-way vibes are needed or it won't work as it should.
A compromise has always been a fudge to stop a fight,
But many times leaves rancour when both parties think they're
    right.
Defending all the assets that have, legally, been got,
Particularly if they have been got without a shot,
Demands a great alertness in a house or in a nation,
Topped up with smiles and handshakes that will form a good
    relation.
A loving way of living must be bonded tight with trust.
No looking over shoulders or a sly sarcastic thrust.
The animal-survival instinct driving what is done
Makes loving situations needing will-power to be won.
Relaxed and steadfast confidence will found the loving care
That forms bulwarks of character resisting those who dare
Upset the forward thinking that will lift the mind above
All petty things that rankle, and pursue a life of love.
Successful living separates the moods of love and passion.
The hope is that the choice will make tranquillity the fashion.

Accidents Waiting to Happen

Go up the road; go down the road –
The perils are the same.
The pavement, the pathetic kerb,
An inch or two from death.
Two lanes opposed with lethal flow.
A vital metal bar
May have its death throe through fatigue.
The traffic noise is king.
The fibres of the metal part
And no one hears the sound,
A snap, a crack, a bang perhaps,
Within a flash it's gone.
The ordered rumble on the tar
Is now a last despair
Of screeching rubber; locked-up wheels,
And pray that gods may spare.

The Statistic

His life went on from childhood to the man.
By chance, retired and quite old,
He rolled his sleeve up, on a sunny day,
And never gave a second thought
That he revealed the story of a century.
For anyone who knew the sign
The clue to bestiality in man
Was there in numbered evidence
To be decoded by the ones who see.
The truth of digits on his arm,
Deep tattooed, marking skin eternally,
Was known to him to keep himself,
For he alone possessed the right to tell.
Between the child and the grown man
A youthful period was black.
His value as a person did not rate.
That he survived: a miracle.
The daily killing made him near insane.
By sheer tenacity of mind,
And luck, his captors had a use for him.
When liberation day arrived,
The cages opened, nightmares left behind,
Or so he hoped. It was not so.
His tattooed arm was not his only scar.
His mind, his soul, his psyche too
All had eternal wounds for him to bear.
A child, in its innocence,
May ask why numbers are upon his arm,
And, if he chose to tell the tale,

How would a fragile mind cope with it all?
He'd probably decide to tell
Another yarn to let the past be past,
And tell the child to build the future fast.

Energy Search

The tidal flow,
The windward blow.
Is this the power of tomorrow?
The burning coal,
The gas store toll.
Is energy a thing to borrow?
There's nothing free
So grow a tree
It's having carbon on the hoof
To soak up CO2
That's made by me and you,
Which has become a worldwide spoof.
Believe, believe in Climate Change?
But is this thought within our range
Of knowledge of these wondrous things?
The Don Quixotes of this world
Still tilt at windmills in the hope
That carbon footprints are reduced,
But how much CO2 has shot
Into the atmosphere we breathe
In manufacturing these piles?
Think nuclear to get the truth
Of generation, carbon free.
It's engineering's urgent plea.

Squirrelwise

I'm nothing but a squirrel
Or, at least, that's what I'm told.
My actual name is Cyril,
So my nickname leaves me cold.
It's true I'm a collector
And I hoard most anything,
A natural inspector,
Rummaging will always bring
A glowing feel with me
If I find a treasure trove,
Which always comes for free,
When I beat the other cove.

It's not a pile of junk.
Useful things have endless life;
Believe it or you're sunk
Into a trap with lots of strife.
Just think of it this way:
Squirrels make the future bright,
They hide and, then, one day
Vital things may come to light
That have been quite forgotten.
Throw away a vital part,
You'll feel distinctly rotten
You don't hoard? Then make a start,
It benefits this way:
Bits you keep may play their part
To really save the day.

RICHARD GARRARD

Ode to a Wounded Knee

Oh knee, oh worthy knee, what hast, I beg,
Brought that which gives me such a lot of pain?
Thy working twin upon the other leg
Doth soldier on to take the extra strain.
What twist or turn hath set thyself on fire
And made each step upon the stair a trial?
I plead forgiveness that I should admire
Your task well done; eternal as time's dial.
I'll give thee rest, if that will form relief,
And smooth the burning area I see
With lotions that will fill me with belief
That soon, with normal movement, I can be
As balanced and as agile as we knew
With thee, dear friend, in painless liberty.
Afrolicking, we three, as if we flew.

Tally-ho!

The chase is more exciting than the kill,
The prey is caught, is dead, is in the pot.
It is consumed, its passing fits the bill,
But chasing needs a strategy and plot.
The hunting instinct never is suppressed,
The word ambition clouds the truthful aim
And losers can't avoid to be distressed
As, come what may, survival is the game.

The chase is more exciting than the kill,
Unless achievement, from the chase, can be
Assessed as notching up the human skill
Without destruction and depravity.
An ideal state, a pipedream to obtain.
The writings of the prophets of the past
Have tried to teach mankind the actual gain,
But, little of their teaching seems to last.

The chase is more exciting than the kill,
Grab what you can along the road of life.
Try, try again until you have your fill
But heed the pitfalls that are all too rife.
Store up the warnings in your memory,
Pick out of file the ones that seem to fit
The situation as it shows to be.
The window of a chance may be a slit.
The chase is more exciting than the kill,
What if the prey is someone else's goal?
The field is narrowed, roads become uphill,
Intensive racing for the cherry bowl

Will test your energies to breaking point.
In every situation that you face
Don't split a gut or twist a vital joint.
Keep focused and control a measured pace.

The chase is more exciting than the kill,
You pounce, the chase is done, the prey is yours.
Now relish every moment of the thrill.
If you should speak with prey within your jaws
It will escape, your secret will be lost.
Cling on and savour your well won success.
Achievement will have worth at any cost,
So, give your soul well-being to excess.

Spring Uprise

We're always told when spring has sprung,
But spring is not a word I use
To rise from bed, get bedclothes flung
Across the room, and thus abuse
The comfort of a night-time nest
So crafted, with the utmost care,
To give the zenith feel of rest.
The morning comes. But who would dare?
This time of year a crisis lies
In wait, towards the end of March,
Intent on ending sweet bye-byes.
But, if you're ready and can starch
The body to resist the call
Of sun-up sixty minutes less,
You will prevent your life from stall
And all your timing in a mess
By putting watch-time on an hour
The night before your bedwise stay.
Whatever time you rise and shower
The truth is what the dial hands say.

Summer Uprise

The hope is: 'summertime is bright.'
It should be hot and sunny.
The bedclothes, normally, are light.
A sticky night: not funny.
When it is ten o'clock at night
And daylight has just done,
The sleeping-time receives a blight,
At five a.m. the sun has won.
Delay the pain of uprise some
With drapes of heavy curtain.
Windows letting more air come
Will make the peace uncertain.
The morning chorus of the birds
Is maddening to say the least;
The use of quite expressive words
Will not deter the breakfast feast.
However much you want to stay
In bed, the tide of time will brush
You into yet another day
That starts with classic hours of rush.

Autumn Uprise

A time to start the winter rest,
In modern parlance called the fall
When many creatures do their best
To find a refuge, and to crawl
Into the safest corner there
To make their hibernation sound
Until the bluebells seek the air
And fresh new food should, then, abound.
But woe the life of humankind:
The temperature is falling fast,
The daily grind is such a bind
That hibernation cannot last
Beyond conventional eight hours.
Then 'up betimes' as, come what may,
The teeth will chatter, spirit cowers,
Olden loyalties begin the day.
The autumn brings an hour more sleep,
And Christmas Day looms up ahead,
So use the hour to count more sheep
And thank the stars you've got a bed.

Winter Uprise

The frost was hard, the bed was soft,
Addicted cowardice took hold.
The frozen tanks up in the loft
Could spell disaster, so I'm told.
Extremes well up in timid souls,
Impossible realities appear,
There is no time for Drake-like bowls,
The peak of feeling is of fear.
Trembling fingers grab the face,
The pillow has magnetic force,
The duvet still controls its space,
The pounding heart spells out in morse,
The adipose is jelled and cowers.
But vibes of bravery make sense:
A toe pokes out with mouse-like powers,
Heroics send the duvet thence.
Triumphant in a freezing room
Will boost the ego on the spot.
A momentary tweak of gloom,
Oh! Is the washing water hot?

Dew-Pond Magic

A boy sat by the pond. What did he see?
His inward vision told exotic tales.
To others: just a toy boat sailing free.
To him: a cloud of newly laundered sails.
A ship defying nature on the sea,
And slicing, with its bow, wave after wave
To reach a destination out of sight
When counting every minute it must save
To catch commercial vantage as of right.
But now the boy has gone. Time made the man.
The pond has lost the use it one-time had,
But it will never change in its lifespan.
Its mystique never heralds what is bad.
The concrete dimples on the southern Downs
Are history that never disappeared.
No sheep to drink, but people from the towns
To dunk their dogs and get their fur bugs cleared.
With flashback over eight decadal years,
The magic vision of the boisterous main
Appears afresh with all exciting fears
As man-made boy is back to live again
The magic of the pond which captures him.
It shuts out pain caused by the getting there –
Exhilaration rules. He's lived a whim
To think of might-of-been with so much flair.
The man becomes his age. The job is done.
He turns away to leave the magic pond.
His birthday treat at ninety has been won.
He drags himself away to break the bond.

Mists of Time

Come to the little cottage down the lane;
The lack of city clatter keeps you sane.
Then think philosophy and feel its spell,
There is a feast of commonsense to tell.
Lay back, absorb the reasoning of old.
Surprise yourself. The logic still is told
That's one-track from the far-off mists of time.
Demand has built a gadget-hill to climb,
And crammed our minds with things that are a 'must',
Which is the true philosophy of lust.

The china shop of morals was quite full
Until the 1960s freed its bull,
Which smashed to smithereens the age-old rules,
And turned the social thinking into mules.
The fences that kept peace in family life
Were trampled down. No freedom there but strife.
The human psyche needs restraint to thrive,
An ordered purpose keeps the flame alive
To show the way to happiness ahead
When enemies transform to friends instead.

But do not wait for theory to be fact
As history is scenes that re-enact.
All pies up in the sky are always off
When ordered, making all the punters scoff.
What promises, as vote-traps, are upheld?
The tree of knowledge starves and soon is felled
And leadership, supposed, will lose its edge.
Which makes the opposition state its pledge
To bring the same good fortune to us all;
But equable society will stall.

State mediocrity will then prevail –
Progression must inevitably fail.
A thousand social orders died the same
When total loss of pride destroyed all shame;
For then, high-minded leadership was lost,
And *laissez-faire* was there at deadly cost.
Eventually some brightness took the stage
When vent was given to frustrated rage,
And those with purpose raised a louder voice
To force the populace to make a choice.

First: positive and forward-looking rule
With stable government that will not fool
The new electorate with unreal dreams.
But flip the coin and fortune brings new themes.
Dictatorships grow mushroom-like in fields
Of surging discontent and anarchy that yields
A seeming saviour with a one-track mind
Who uses brainwash tactics aimed to bind
The will of masses; form a national course
To scare the neighbours with aggressive force.

What's Justice if advantage is not fair?
The just among us are supposed to care.
The unjust has the notion to ignore
The plight of those who knock upon his door.
The conscience is a complicated thing,
It's satisfied with ethics on a string
To pull each which-way as to mould the mind
Into beliefs of cults of every kind.
When conscience accepts prejudice as norm
Disregarding metaphysics as reform.

Cast out the Individual as fact.
Proceed to give to every one a tract

Which is a scripture that portrays a truth
To capture thinking of a nation's youth.
To straighten conscience and to make it strong
For helping mankind to know right from wrong,
Has always been a 'grey-cell-sorting' task
As every outside show will wear a mask.
The privacy of thought is guaranteed,
But thinking what is right will need a creed.

Help 'harmlessness' to make a firm resolve
Which rains of ridicule will not dissolve.
A wrongful thought makes headway very fast,
Its very speed will cause it not to last.
Salvation for the human soul is where
The happy conscience always votes for 'FAIR'.
Philosophical behaviour, of a kind,
Will always occupy the human mind
To harness all the power that can be used.
Think on! Your shattered egos will be fused.

Food Economics

It's not the food that makes you fat.
It's not the drink that makes you drunk.
It is the quantity. That's that.
A diet is a load of bunk.
Why spend a lot on surplus fuel?
Equate the workload with the need.
Your taste buds will be very cruel
And goad and tempt you to exceed
The adipose you carry round
Which stresses hips and knees and feet,
Until you find that, pound on pound,
Will make you glad to take a seat.
To run would make your poor heart pump,
So, cut the fuel and exercise
Before you are a great fat lump.
It works. Go to. Have a surprise.

The Risk Vibes

The Chinese whispers travel far and wide.
Mock secrecy designed to stir the pot
With no pretence to really try to hide
Discreditable comments that will blot
The character, mischievously, of one
Who will not be aware of future strife,
Or conscious of the damage that is done
To social living and the working life.
Now, double Dutch is rarely understood,
A well-known subtle way to form a code.
It sounds like nonsense from a mind of wood,
But skill will change it to deciphered mode.
And gobbledegook is rubbish to the ear.
'Intelligence', a word for world know-how,
Can fill you with exaggerated fear.
Reality is just the here and now.

The purpose of this piece is to remind
The rest of us how others can deceive.
So watch your back for those who are unkind
And look out for the tangles that they weave.

Marbles

'Just where are my glasses?' the old man said,
'I'm sure that I had them when I was in bed,
I'll just have to manage with the old ones instead.
Ah! Now I remember; when I sliced the bread
I thought they were draped round my neck on a thread.
Oh dear; if they're dropped I must watch where I tread.'
'You only have one pair,' the young man said,
'You're getting forgetful like old Uncle Fred.'
The old man, indignant, 'He went off his head.
I'd rather you thought I was like my friend Ned,
He's got all his marbles, but sometimes sees red
If anyone tells him he ought to be dead;
They joke that he's ninety and should not be fed.'
The young man daren't say that he's losing his cred.
It's the one thing the old man is certain to dread.
His ego would drop like a ton of old lead.
He is very old and some memories have fled,
But remembers, in detail, the day he was wed.
His anger boils up about his brother Ted –
And his part in how family assets were bled.

The glasses were found on the top of his head.
His psyche was hurt by not one single shred.
You'd best take a breath after what you have read.

Philomel

The songs of praise and songs of hate
Have always plagued humanity,
But often they have sealed the fate
Of those with hyped-up vanity.
A patriotic anthem will
Give lift when danger's in the air
As it has words designed to fill
A country's heart and kill despair.
The thrills that come from Philomel
Give magic to the atmosphere
And lyrically cast a spell
That's truly music to the ear.
They're packed with warning and with joy,
It's nature's diva in a tree,
And does not tire and does not cloy,
But envy reigns for flying free.
Its feathered cousins need no words,
And join the chorus in the sky
To let us understand the birds
Who raise our spirits up so high.

Ponderation

To ruminate or chew the cud
Will pan the gold out of the mud,
It exercises mind and jaw
And leads the way to more and more.
Enlightenment will tune the bent
And store your future nourishment.
To hurry thought spells its decline
And kills the vintage of the wine;
The bouquet suffers and the gain
Is lost forever from the brain.
What great ideas, when newly born,
Will leave the genius forlorn?
Because the world was blind to see,
You can't get wood without a tree.
All radical inventions need
To be thought through before the seed
Will blossom for the greater good,
And serve the purpose that it should.

Evolution: Or is it?

Original Adams: original Eves
Stood in a brand-new wonderland.
The Big Bang done, the sun received
Its role to run the earthly brand.
Assume a start, assume an end.
But is not space-time infinite?
With instinct, living things attend
To all things being definite.
But Adam, Eve and company
Looked prospect fully in the face,
And with a rousing timpani
Dictated 'future's aim and pace'
A mere existence quickly bored.
Improve, improve, invent, invent.
Try this, try that. Then, knowledge stored
Made all the time it took well spent,
But human generation span
Has always been an eye-wink long.

Each person's contribution can
Make only what is there more strong.
A billion millennium years
Made progress in a notch-like way
With two steps on: one back with tears.
The surge that makes the daily sway.
From this regime traditions grow;
It's when real progress takes a knock.
Then some will think that life's too slow
And up a gear of man's own clock.
With Big Bang two, tradition went.
The sprinting sciences were king
And new inventiveness was bent

On phasing out the human 'thing'.
The 'future'. What a dream is there?
Control the climate? What a hope.
The sun instructs, and that is where
Ingeniousness will learn to cope.

To level blame for climate change
At necessary human life
Is scientifically strange,
But politicians make it rife
To build up guilt in public mind
And pave the way to penal tax;
But most of CO2, you'll find,
Comes from our breathing. Check the facts.
World chemistry was so designed
To process variants galore.
But let us not be too resigned.
Keep local air from being poor.
The galaxy in constant change
Has happened all the earth's long life.
From ice to drought. Back through the range,
It's always been a world of strife.
But should the sun put out the light,
The job of planet earth is done.
How, then, will Adam use his sight
To judge the value that was won?
And when he sees it ends in NOWT,
He'll say, 'What was it all about?'

The Floral Chance?

There was a time when Heather was my friend,
But Iris lured me to her side instead.
The loveliness of Rose made all that end
Till Daisy, one fine day, popped up her head.
My will was weak when Violet appeared,
But Clementine had overwhelming charm.
Then Myrtle came and my love-patch was queered;
But not for long when Lily took my arm.
By then I thought that Jasmine was for me,
But Rosemary was well ahead, and then
It was sweet Hyacinth who set me free.
Confusion came with Primrose in my ken.

Oh Marguerite, why did you run away?
You left a void which Lavender jumped in
When Honeysuckle hoped to make her day.
Then May turned up and had a chance to win.
Now Zinnia loomed beautiful and young
When Peony, with poise and gentle grace,
Joined with Veronica to tie my tongue.
I feared a Wallflower as the last disgrace.
Then Kate, although her name was not a flower,
She beat the lot of them at floral power.
And so it is and hope will always be,
But payback time will need returns from me.

Insomnia

Along the way, the other day,
I met a man who loses sleep.
When he's in bed he tries to play
Imagined games, or counting sheep
With hope to lose the daily grind.
He'd tried all kinds of sleeping pill
But, still, his overactive mind
Clicks back to day against his will.
I was devoid of sound advice
As sleep comes easily to me.
I said 'I know of no device
That brings on sleep quite easily.
There is one trick that I have used
That brings on mild tranquillity,
And it is not to get well boozed,
But everyone's ability
Can raise their cheeks and form a smile.
Just close the eyes and blank the brain,
Relax the body. That's the style.
It may just work. You'll sleep again.'
I hope, for him, it is the way
His problem eased, the other day.

Blandness

Along the way, the other day
I met a man who had no taste,
Not in a kind of fashion way,
But *haute cuisine*, to him, is waste.
He loves to eat a hearty meal,
But texture is his only guide,
With presentation that is real,
To eat the food and then provide
Appreciation to the cook
Avoiding asking what he had
Without a questionable look
As if he thought the food was bad.
With taste is coupled sense of smell.
To him the most exotic rose
Lacks any scent that he can tell,
But, with no feel in tongue or nose,
He is not tempted nor acquires
Addictions for unhealthy food.
He eats no more than he requires
To keep himself in happy mood.
My admiration went his way
As I felt blessed, the other day.

Spite

Have hurtful sayings plagued your life?
Then slam the doors on memory.
Use windows on the sunny side
To futurise your time that's left.
Leave all the nastiness behind.
Make every moment fill with joy.
There will be people you can trust,
So clear your thoughts of those who scar
Your mind with mischief meant to hurt.
Their pleasure must be thrown aside.
You'll feel refreshed with your new life.
With head held high you'll shrug off strife.

Colour Trap

Along the way, the other day
A friend I met is colour-blind.
He's often asked me not to say
To others who may be unkind.
He suffered bullying at school,
And there is work outside his scope
Where colour-coding is the tool.
He always feels he has no hope
Of getting mobile with a car.
The traffic-lights should not confuse –
The only thing to cause trauma
Is change of sequence that they use.
He knows the top is always red,
The bottom light is always green.
He's got this fixed within his head,
But trust is mixed with what he's seen.
The way he copes with 'come-what-may'
Called for respect, the other day.

Grit

I am just a grain of sand
In the desert of mankind.
Outsize boots of government
Force, with every heavy tread,
Countless grains, without their will,
Changes to a pressured mass
Blocked against the winds that blow
Grains that are quite free to whirl,
Choosing from a range of dunes
Showing that they're not the same.
Talent that is never used
Falls into the sands of time.
All at once a grain stands out,
Gets the desert on its side,
Wearing boots that help our path.
Just a grain of sand like us,
Ground into a different shape,
Having facets that will count,
Dealing with the endless strife,
Trudging through the sands of life.

Memory

Along the way, the other day,
I met a man who'd lost his way.
He did not know which way to go.
His real confusion went to show
That age was probably the cause
For his 'short memory' to pause.
I said hallo and asked his name.
His face displayed a type of shame;
To think that he was not aware
Of who he was brought on a stare
That, slowly, indicated fear.
Then, suddenly, a sound, quite near,
Gave him a memory of school.
It acted like a magic tool
To switch his time-clock into NOW
And clear his mind to show him how
He could relate to playground shouts
To tell him he lived thereabouts.
Then, all at once, he said, 'I'm Bill,
I live at sixteen, up the hill.'
I helped him home to his own door.
His wife was much relieved, but saw
Alzheimer's may be on the way.
I'm glad I helped, the other day.

Blind Man's Bluff

Along the way, the other day,
I saw a man who could not see.
To help him not to go astray,
And make his forward pathway free,
He swept his stick from left to right
To warn the people, dead ahead,
That he was without normal sight.
Anxiety filled me with dread
As he approached the pavement edge.
I went to him to lend a hand
He said, 'No thanks, I've made a pledge
To suffer blindness. I have planned
A day of being without eyes
So that I have the pent-up feel
Of constant darkness as time flies
The horror that it may be real.'
His blindfold was securely fixed.
He wanted me to go with him
To show me how sounds can get mixed,
Which goes to danger life and limb.
'I am in shock to find how well
The sightless people face their lives.'
I hope his tests will really tell
Him information that he strives.
As he left me and walked away
It humbled me, the other day.

Part 4

Qui Vive?

She said that she would love me till I die.
A prospect that needs thought of every kind.
What timescale has she got? think I –
A normal span of years? Or will I find
There is a shorter time to contemplate.
I love her deeply and would give my all,
But all I have will never make a spate.
I hope my death will be a natural call.
If odds are laid, she might go on ahead,
And I may be the cat that gets the cream;
But that is something that I really dread.
Should I be left alone I'd only scream,
For loneliness is nothing I would wish.
I'd wither like an out-of-water fish.

Hail St George

Meandering along the garden path
I breathed the scent of everything that grows.
The scene of beauty is the aftermath
Of skill and toil by everyone who knows
The secret habits of all plants and more.
Then through a gated arch I held my breath.
A fountain that I had not seen before
Transfixed my mind to only think of death.
A statue of a knight about to thrust
The final cut into a dragon's heart
With all the venom of a warrior's lust.
And then the penny dropped. It was a start
To show that setbacks, like symbolic rain,
Will never stop the Brits from making gain.

Passing Phase

The beauty that is yours is not surpassed.
Search high and low I'm sure I'll never see
Such symmetry which was not in the past.
You are a standard for eternity.
Your gliding walk has grace and poise galore,
The lightness of your steps, with fairy feet,
Kid me I've seen it all; my eyes find more.
The elements of all this beauty meet
To awe beholders of the female form.
You make a model of exquisite charm.
If I look more my blood will start to warm
And that will do our friendship lasting harm.
With mind set on a straight and thinking course,
When beauty's gone, there's no need for remorse.

Love-Struck

I see her walking in the morning air,
The early sunrise loses out in glory.
I cannot move, but only stand and stare.
My fantasising mind makes up a story.
To be beside her is an endless dream.
Her voice can only be the sound of love.
The zephyrs through the roses near the stream
Give perfumes that are hers, from heaven above.
The grace and poise make music through my eyes,
A love-drenched theme will come into my mind.
If only I can make her realise
How passionate I feel, and she would find
Her life with me, filled with devoted love,
Would be as peaceful as the cooing dove.

Perspective

It is the most delightful thing I know,
Just sitting with you shaded by this tree,
To hear your tales of happiness and woe
That span your life as captive and when free.
You tell of childhood scampers in this wood,
And then the cloud of war that stopped it all.
With peace, the scene recovered, as it should,
As nature brought back springtime and the fall.
The depth of understanding you express
Has drawn perspective that will never fade.
You seem to handle joy and great distress
As though it is the way a life is made.
With triple times more life, you've had, than me
I'll wait to tell my life, back here, times three.

Heart's Change

Why can't you understand I love another.
It's something I must make you comprehend.
You'll only work yourself into a pother
By hanging on to something that won't mend.
The reason why we never were a team
Is your great need to, always, have your way.
I know, to you, my need for space would seem
My inability to give up play;
But, as I am, there's much more give and take,
More true affection stemmed from deep respect,
Which gels into an item that will make
The future have a rosier aspect.
With all my heart, I wish you every joy.
Desist in treating someone as a toy.

Maturity

Sweetheart, please stop those tricks that you contrive
That make me think you're younger than I know.
I love you as you are, you're so alive.
Your youthful attitude will never go
And never be confined to history.
Your smile, with eyes that have eternal light
Like twinkling stars, they always comfort me.
There's no need, any more, to fly a kite
To get my full attention, as you did.
My mind's eye's ever printed with your face
That has matured with gracefulness amid
The toils of life without an ageing trace.
Let me come close and stroke your lovely hair
And feel the warmth that makes our senses flare.

Bliss

You are so cosy. Night-time is a joy.
You are so slim and gorgeous lying there;
I pop to bed, but feel a little coy.
The cuddly world dispels my every care.
There was a time when I did hate your kind
As they were bulky: not at all my type.
But having you has made me change my mind.
The dread of overheating I can wipe
From the anxieties I had of old
And sleep is not disturbed, as in the past,
For now, I'm not too hot and not too cold,
Enjoying blissfulness, in bed, at last.
Hurrah for night-time free of every fear.
Dear Duvet, many thanks for being here.

Phoenix

'Completely useless and a waste of space.'
Not quite the best remark for your CV.
It made me feel below the human race,
But, in a funny way, it set me free.
I had to rethink how I used my days.
Reduce by one the country's human glut?
Then search my skills to make me mend my ways,
To transform 'layabout' to 'social strut'.
With one year on, she's had to change her mind,
And wants me back to share my new-found wealth.
Oh no! I've found a new way to unwind
As, back to her would jeopardise my health;
But sweetness in a life is not all money,
So now I'm looking for a little honey.

Angel Sound

That voice, that voice, just once I heard that voice.
My mind did somersaults, my heart joined in:
And from that moment there was not a choice.
My life was focused and I had to win
The earthbound angel who had probed my-soul
And fired emotions I'd not known before.
There was no time to waste to win this goal,
For hesitation meant I'd never score.
I don't remember how I asked her out;
My blood rushed to my head. I fell in love.
I wanted to go mad and cheer and shout
And hope my luck had come from heaven above.
Some sixty-seven years have passed us by,
So full of loving that they seemed to fly.

Poetic Licence

A lovely garden is romanced about.
Great poets conjure up a peaceful scene:
'The glory of a garden' is the shout.
They try to make you feel that you have been
And feasted boggled eyes at nature's trim.
How many of them have those aching backs
Through digging down to fill up, to the brim,
Those borders with displays that nothing lacks?
The planting out can be a tedious toil,
And getting velvet lawns is no mean task,
But satisfying work to men of soil.
The poets in their fantasy should ask
How beauty is created out of dirt.
And join the workforce in a sweaty shirt.

Grooming

A child stood at the corner of the street
Bewildered by the human surge and pace.
Its lamb-like face appeared to make a bleat,
'Please help me with the troubles I shall face.'
The hurdles of an education loom,
The trials and tribulations of exams,
And all along the way the moral broom
Is working overtime to sweep the jams
Of rubbish in the river of a life;
The rubbish that erodes the banks, unseen,
Until the mainstream slows with widened strife
And kills the future making 'might-have-been'.
A child well grown and tended like a flower
Will bring a harvest full of strength and power.

Sound Bites

All written words are marks upon a page,
Their music is transformed by every tongue
That demonstrates a temper, calm or rage.
What joy to hear a person, very young,
Interpret what they see into a sound.
The fact that many languages prevail
Provides a mystery that is profound,
And yet the nations have this worded veil
Preventing understanding face to face,
Thus causing conflict through the act of speech,
Obstructing clarity in every case.
Words talking is the only way to reach
The inner feelings of a person's mind,
So cherish sound-biting of every kind.

The Big Cleanse

Let's wash it all away and clean the world.
We'll clear the slate, abolish history.
Give thought to straighten every thing that's curled
And clarify the cult of mystery.
Wash down the throat with water, not with booze.
Scrub from the mind well-known corruptive thought
That rots the brain to cause distressing ooze
With which addictions and bad health are bought.
'Come clean' is said when they demand the facts.
'Clean up your act' or 'organise yourself'.
Go forth and see if all the world reacts
To clear the dust and dirt from every shelf.
A new start is a dream that seems too good,
But nice to see the world run as it should.

Testy

'Now try that new manoeuvre once again,
You have to stop the car from running back.
The whole point of the thing is to obtain
Coordination that you seem to lack'.
'Don't tell me all the things I cannot do,
I'm paying you to get me through the test,
You'll next be saying I'm a silly moo' . . .
'Oh no! I'm sure you do your very best.
So now go through the normal pedal drill.
We're off. Keep on until we reach the top,
And then first right as we come down the hill.
First right! You've missed the turn. For God's sake stop.
Not crash it! Now you've put the car to bed.
You'd better buy some walking shoes instead.'

Thrift

He said I spent too much on every dress.
I thought that he would like me to be smart.
He'd soon complain if I looked like a mess
Or Annie who he always calls a tart.
I think I know how I can pull his leg:
I'll turn to charities and search their shops
To find designer labels off the peg
And see if he will comment when he mops
His brow at my apparent wastefulness.
He'll ask to see my credit card account
To try to cost my new-found tastefulness.
I know he won't make sense of the amount,
And when I've had my fun I'll tell the lot;
But he'll take credit for the wife he's got.

Horror

The other night I saw a dreadful thing.
The aftershock disturbs my normal sleep.
In daytime it is difficult to bring
A calmness that will let me try to sweep
The memory of agony galore
Away from daily doing of my work.
The horror of dismemberment and gore
Gives flashed-up pictures full of frightful murk.
With hindsight it is shocking to believe
That such depravity is carried out
In public view with nothing to relieve
The tension that this horror brings about.
In future, to avoid a massive scare,
I must select my cinema with care.

Illusion

I thought I saw a mermaid in the sea,
The trailing locks, the graceful forward glide.
I was transfixed with all there seemed to be,
But wondered what the mermaid had to hide.
As she emerged and left the sea behind
I held my breath. She had no fish's tail.
She had the natural beauty of her kind
With shapeliness and poise that cannot fail.
I helped her up the beach and found a chair.
'I thought you were a mermaid at first sight'.
'Go on! I'd still be floundering out there,
I'll stick to legs, if that will be all right.'
Her company was all that I could wish.
Perhaps that's why I'm very fond of fish.

Taken Chance

She stood, with many others, in a shop
And every time I passed she was still there;
So, in the end my instincts made me stop
Because my looking had become a stare.
I was quite mesmerised by what I saw,
Against my better judgement I went in
And broke the ice with idle chat, and more.
I bravely asked, with hope that I may win,
If she could come upon a little trip;
Although it meant it was a working lunch.
We went. I really had to get a grip
Of my emotions, as I had a hunch
That I had just fulfilled a lovely dream
And bought a motor car that was the cream.

Dreamland

Last night I dreamt the sweetest dreams of you.
It was about your funny little ways.
You cutely tweaked your nose and smiled too.
The way you walked did nothing but amaze.
I loved the way you giggled at my jokes,
You even made me think that I could dance
Much better, in this place, than other blokes.
The whole of me was whipped into a trance
By your coquettishness and sultry voice.
But just as we were getting very close
I sprang awake and had not any choice
From getting up to take my daily dose
Of pulling pints behind this dreary bar;
When you come in it changes to five star.

Graduation

A sea of mortarboards were in the church.
The day had come to celebrate success.
Supporters jostled in their frantic search
To get a glimpse of one that they possess.
Excited prattle filled the atmosphere.
The concourse came to order at a call
To ask the congregation to revere
Processing academics to their stall.
The precious paper scrolls were held in pride
As graduates filed out to celebrate
The joyousness impossible to hide.
Though all will have a life to contemplate,
But first, to end a most exciting day,
A cloud of mortarboards went up in play.

Nonagenarianism

I mourn the past; but was it right or not?
There is no way to make the question valid.
My social order doesn't mean a jot.
The face of history becomes more pallid,
But then, each generation has its way
Of living and adjusting old tradition.
Most people, now, can broadcast what they say
And reassess their meaning of perdition.
More lives are frittered on a daily base
With no investment for the pastures new.
Stability should be a winning race
For everyone and not the lucky few.
But there's no need to live just on your wits,
Though past is past, it holds great benefits.

Beware

I hope I never do what I regret.
The nuances of life can catch you out.
Misunderstandings often make folk fret,
An agitated conscience makes them shout.
A blush is often noticed as a sign
That, oops! a word or two have touched a nerve
Which puts morale and wits into decline,
Upsetting all the confidence and verve
That may have dressed the surface for the world.
Hear this! 'Be sure your sins will find you In.'
A motto which is usefully unfurled
To anyone who thinks their wrongs will win.
A tricky situation needs the legs
That have dexterity to walk on eggs.

Worth

Unravel in your mind what value means.
Is like or dislike flavouring the choice?
A must-have element is what it seems.
With merchandise, will auction have a voice?
A talismanic bonding has some worth.
A kindly act is priceless at the time,
Think how you put a price upon a birth.
What element will make a life sublime?
'You can't buy happiness' is somewhat trite;
But wealth will, surely, give a helping hand,
Though not if human vibes lose all their might
And jealousies destroy a wonderland.
Take heart. True worth is in the way we live
That benefits from empathy we give.

Luck?

It was an accident that did the trick.
My heel got caught between two paving stones.
Three men gave help, but one was very quick
To see that, as I fell, I'd broken bones.
My time in hospital was fairly short.
I left today and saw a man go by
Who flashed my mind, although I only caught
A fleeting glimpse that made me really try
To add some detail to my picture-mind;
And then I got it, clear in every way.
In cap and gown, this man who was so kind
To fix my breaks, and did not give away
An inkling that he had a shine for me
Has left his number on my leg. Whoopee!

What Price Modernity?

Let's smile and laugh away the worldwide gloom.
There's negativity like heavy fog,
Which tells the psyche of approaching doom.
The stresses that go with the daily slog
Bring social chaos in the strive for wealth
And kill the many pleasant things of life.
Modernity has jeopardised the health
Of all art forms. It's hacking with a knife
To slash at thought and find there's nothing there.
A renaissance in discipline and skill
Is shouting to be heard to make folk care,
When given chances to express the will
To tag modernity 'a loaded curse'
And give life back to painting, music, verse.

My Hero

Wherever you may go I must go too.
My soul feeds on the vibes you emanate.
My peace of mind will make me bill and coo,
Although I know that this is what you hate.
I long to shadow you for every day
And bask in intellectual utterance.
The food for thought in everything you say
Can be so heady, in the circumstance.
That mental indigestion grabs my brain
And hero-worship overtakes good sense.
It's then that strength of will makes me restrain
Embarrassing emotional pretence.
To keep our friendship buoyant without fault
I'll bring the hero-worship to a halt.

Faithless

My God did not desert me. I lost faith.
Religion is a waiting game for most:
A timeless hope for everlasting rathe;
A happy chance to join the heavenly host.
A deity is like a straw to grab,
It gives great comfort and a peace of mind
To those who find their daily life is drab.
But, over years of wondering, I find
That when I pray I'm talking to myself.
The supernatural is not for me.
I took reality down from the shelf
To put religion there to set me free.
My peace of mind protects me from a wraith.
My God did not desert me. I lost faith.

Divine Food

Ambrosia, the name of food for gods,
And nectar is the drink to complement.
The menu that compares for earthly bods
Needs bags of earthly cash to implement,
But that depends on fashion of the day.
Seafood was, once, for peasants, and was free,
And turkey was an *haute cuisine* display.
Reverse availability and see
How pricing really influences fad.
Don't envy gods for being gastronomes.
I'm sure that they would only be too glad
To have a cup-o-char in earthly homes,
Or have a taste of bacon on their lips,
But, best of all, they'd relish fish and chips.

Aimlessness

That boredom is a self-inflicted wound
Should give a hint to get the brain in gear
And force the tree of life to be well pruned
So making objectivity more clear.
Exotic living is devoid of aim.
A ravished body looms as the result.
But idleness feeds boredom just the same.
Only an inner spring will catapult
New mental missiles that will change a life
And launch the mind into activity,
Which will dispel a mass of self-made strife
With improved sense of relativity.
Including those whose life is silver-spooned,
All boredom is a self-inflicted wound.

Oops!

Of course I'm soaking wet, it's pouring down.
What have I done that you won't let me in?
The party! Yes, I guess I was a clown.
A bit of boisterousness is not a sin.
I thought you liked a cuddle in the dark;
You certainly enjoyed it at the time.
But can't you see, the whole thing was a lark,
I have to say I found it quite sublime.
Please open up, I'll get my death of cold,
Then where will all our future planning go?
We'll laugh at this when we are very old.
All right, but first there's something you must know:
You were so sozzled that you could not see
The one you slobbered over wasn't me.

RICHARD GARRARD

Waiting for Bliss

'How long have we been waiting at this spot?
She said she would be here at six o'clock.'
'She usually comes here on the dot;
I'll wait a little longer then take stock.
You two go on and get a decent seat,
We'll have to take pot luck when we arrive.'
'OK, ta-ta! I hope that we shall meet –
The crush looks like we'll struggle to survive.'
They left. I saw her standing in the shade.
'You minx. Your witchcraft made them go away,
So now, it seems, we've really got it made
To gather up our time and use in play.
Apply our mutual love to set us free
For amorously intertwining spree.'

Be Mine

Beloved is the word I have for thee.
Thy shadow is enough to show the flower.
The gracefulness of movement that I see
Makes zephyrs wafting me unto thy bower.
The goddesses of ancient times are shamed
Compared to sculptured beauty that is thine.
The cupid's arrows that mine eyes have aimed
Are tributes to thy loveliness divine.
To win thy heart would be a golden prize.
A fire of passion, brighter than the sun,
Would burn within me; fill me with surprise
That such exotic feelings could be won.
May time mature my thoughts within thy mind,
And pray that Lady Luck is not unkind.